SOLDIER ON!

THE TESTAMENT OF A TOM

Joe Starling

Foreword by
Major General Michael Walsh CB, DSO, DL

SPELLMOUNT LTD
Tunbridge Wells · Kent

Published in the UK in 1992 by
Spellmount Ltd
12 Dene Way, Speldhurst
Tunbridge Wells, Kent TN3 0NX

A catalogue record for this book is available
from the British Library

ISBN 0-946771-36-7

© Brigadier J.G. Starling 1992

All rights reserved. No part of this publication
may be reproduced, stored in a retrieval system
or transmitted in any form or by any means,
electronic, mechanical, photocopying, recording or
otherwise, without prior permission in writing
from Spellmount Ltd, Publishers.

Typeset by Vitaset, Paddock Wood, Kent
Printed by The Ipswich Book Co Ltd, Ipswich, Suffolk

Contents

In the Spellmount/Nutshell Military list:

The Territorial Battalions – A pictorial history
The Yeomanry Regiments – A pictorial history
Over the Rhine – The Last Days of War in Europe
History of the Cambridge University OTC
Yeoman Service
The Fighting Troops of the Austro-Hungarian Army
Intelligence Officer in the Peninsula
The Scottish Regiments – A pictorial history
The Royal Marines – A pictorial history
The Royal Tank Regiment – A pictorial history
The Irish Regiments – A pictorial history
British Sieges of the Peninsular War
Victoria's Victories
Heaven and Hell – German paratroop war diary
Rorke's Drift
Came the Dawn – Fifty years an Army Officer
Kitchener's Army – A pictorial history
On the Word of Command – A pictorial history of the Regimental Sergeant Major
Marlborough – as Military Commander
The Art of Warfare in the Age of Marlborough
Epilogue in Burma 1945-48
Scandinavian Misadventure
The Fall of France
The First Victory – O'Connor's Desert Triumph Dec 1940-Feb 1941
Blitz Over Britain
Deceivers Ever – Memoirs of a Camouflage Officer
Indian Army of the Empress – 1861-1903
Waters of Oblivion – The British Invasion of the River Plate 1806-07
The French are Coming – The Invasion Scare 1803-05
Heroes for Victoria 1837-1901
Commando Diary
Craufurd's Light Division

In the Military Machine list:

Napoleon's Military Machine
Falklands Military Machine
Wellington's Military Machine

In the Nautical list:

Sea of Memories
Evolution of Engineering in the Royal Navy Vol I 1827-1939
In Perilous Seas

In the Aviation list:

Diary of a Bomb Aimer
Operation 'Bograt' – From France to Burma – Memoirs of a Fighter Pilot
A Medal for Life – Capt Leefe Robinson VC
Three Decades a Pilot – The Third Generation
Bob Doe – Fighter Pilot
The Allied Bomber War 1939-45

Foreword

by
Major General Michael J.H. Walsh CB, DSO, DL

It is sometimes said by officers and NCOs, and by soldiers too, that there are no 'characters' left in the Army of today. Brigadier 'Joe' Starling CBE, MC, DL, is proof that this is not so!

Joe Starling is one of our finest post-war Regimental soldiers of his generation. He was commissioned from Sandhurst into the Suffolk Regiment in 1948 and posted almost immediately to the 1st Battalion in Greece. Shortly afterwards the Battalion was moved to Malaya where it was deployed in Company locations on rubber estates and in small towns such as Kajang in the State of Selangor. It was here that Joe Starling won his Military Cross. His Battalion became renowned for their skill in the jungle and at the end of their three year operational tour were credited with more 'bandit' kills than any other Battalion except 1/2 (KEO) Goorkha Rifles.

It was during this time that I first met Joe Starling. He was sent home to England to be invested by King George VI with his decoration and to attend the Platoon Weapons Course at the Small Arms School at Hythe where, at that time, I was serving as an Instructor. His outstanding leadership qualities which were evident then, both on operations and on training, have remained with him ever since.

I next met up with Joe when I took command of the 1st Battalion The Parachute Regiment in Aldershot shortly before we left on an operational tour to Aden. We trained hard for this arms plot move – not knowing just exactly what role we would have to play. 'Everything under the sun' was the warning as we practised our IA Drills, our set piece Battalion in defence and withdrawal – for we were fairly sure, even at that stage that we would be the last Battation out of Aden. So it proved to be. Joe was my Second-in-Command both in this preparatory stage and throughout the seven months that we were to remain in Aden – described by Kipling as an 'old barrack room stove'. What the 'Toms' of 1 PARA called it, together with the fly-blown tented 'Radfan Camp' which was our home, I dread to think!

Joe played a major role making effective the many operational decisions that I had to take throughout an ever-changing political and military situation. He ensured that our positions in Sheik Othman, such as Fort Walsh, were secure. He personally checked, at some risk, that all our Check Points were resupplied. His land rover toured Area North daily and he always ensured that those who came under command, be they Army, RAF Regiment, Royal Marine Commando, Police, Special Branch or Service Women Searchers, were correctly briefed and looked after. He will always be remembered for his brilliant concept for the protection of the Police Station Tower in Sheik Othman – Joe tells the story within this book.

To be successful there must, I believe, be a special friendship between a Commanding Officer and his Second-in-Command. I shall never forget Joe sending me off by air to visit Dhala, a hill station some hundred miles north of Aden. This was to give me a day's break, a change of scene and, hopefully, a good lunch in a well-renowned Rest House. We both knew that we were to withdraw from Dhala in a few weeks time; so this was the last opportunity. Off I went leaving Joe 'in command'. I remember that there were no incidents in the Log nor marked on the map in the Battalion Ops Room when I left. All was quiet. I spent a good day up country and returned that evening refreshed. On the final approach to RAF Khormaksar, my Army Air Corps Beaver passed over Sheik Othman. Looking down I noticed clouds of smoke coming from the Town and army vehicles racing up the Causeway. On touch down I was met by my land-rover crew. The first words of my signaller, Corporal Coughtree, were 'There is a General Strike in Aden, trouble in Daar Said and Sheik Othman is in flames. Major Starling has just sent this message as you were taxi-ing in: "Tell Sunray not to worry, I have it all under control!" Oh yes Sir, he added that he hopes you had a good day!'

I am sure all soldiers will enjoy reading this book. It is written about them and for them in a style which they will understand and appreciate. Brigadier 'Joe' is first and foremost a Regimental soldier. He has in his 35 years in the Army commanded National Servicemen, regular soldiers, 'Jocks' for whom he has a special affection, and Territorials.

Finally, it is no surprise that in his 'Epilogue' he pays tribute to Army wives and to the British soldier. Joe has been fortunate in having a most loyal and supportive wife. Readers will soon discover that Iris has had to put up with a great deal of separation! Those who have been privileged to know the Starlings will agree that, as a couple, they are a prime example of Regimental and family loyalty being 'one of the principal strengths of the British Army'.

Michael Walsh

DEDICATION
To IRIS,
who has supported me
through thick and thin.

CARTOON ACKNOWLEDGEMENT
The cartoons have been culled from a variety of publications,
whose origin is not known. They seemed worth sharing
and hence have been included in this book.
The author is most grateful for the creative ideas of the
artists and happily acknowledges their contribution.

1

The Start Line

The scene is 10 Downing Street one winter's day in 1946. 'Fred,' said the Prime Minister, 'I want you, as Minister for War, to democratise the Army. The old idea of the officers coming from one social class is way out of date now we have National Service, with a citizen army a million strong. Every young man of ability should have the chance of a commission whatever his background – maybe some of them will even be grateful enough to vote Labour – and while you're at it, let's get rid of the distinction between the 'gentlemen' of the Cavalry and Infantry, who are Sandhurst trained, and the 'players' of the technical Corps at Woolwich. Put the whole lot together.'

'The army brass won't like it, Clem,' replied the War Minister. 'They keep banging on about wanting to get back to real soldiering, now the war is over.' 'Rubbish,' said the PM. 'You and I have both served in a World War. We have seen officers from all walks of life commanding successfully in battle. This is no time for a retrograde step. If the generals don't like it, retire them. We've got too many anyway.'

So the concept of the modern Sandhurst intake was born and, to be fair to its progenitors, has proved remarkably successful over more than forty years. Only one thing did they get wrong. The army thrives on its traditions, regimental pride, service to the nation and loyalty to the Crown. Young people of all ranks are judiciously introduced to the glorious history of their military forbears with the implication that if they do half as well, they will be doing a good job. They are encouraged to do things the way their predecessors did in matters ceremonial and traditional, albeit they also keep right up to date on the tactical aspects of modern war.

The Sergeants' Mess is even more traditional in its outlook. It

1

regards itself, with good reason, as the backbone of the regiment, thriving on the responsibility entrusted to it. No other army in the world, except perhaps those of the old Commonwealth who retain their former British traditions, can hold a candle to the strength and cohesion which a strong Sergeants' Mess provides.

This emphasis on tradition is effectively another name for conservatism with a large or small c, according to individual taste. It is rare indeed to find any member of either an Officers' or Sergeants' Mess who finds socialism appealing.

The army strives to achieve excellence. Levelling down, rather than up, forms no part of their philosophy. It takes a year or two of service – or perhaps a traumatic experience like serving in a war, to inculcate the fierce pride in Regiment and, less directly, country. Some find it difficult to articulate, particularly since patriotism is something of a suspect word in the nineteen nineties, but they believe in it nonetheless. The proof is in the way the Army has conducted its affairs in the many small wars during the retreat from Empire, the Falklands, the Gulf and the continuing, seemingly endless conflict in Northern Ireland. The British Army, small as it is, is the envy of the military of the world. The recurring theme of virtually all military tales is the enduring humour, patience, initiative and courage of the British Soldier.

The post-war generation has adapted Kipling's traditional 'Thomas Atkins' and shortened it to the simple word 'Tom', applied to all save those whose north of the border origin demands that they stick to the equally traditional term 'Jock'.

The Army at large refers to its troops as 'Toms' and what follows are excerpts from the life of one of them, both in the United Kingdom and during some of what the media regard as the 'savage wars of peace'.

2

Early Days

HOW D'YOUSE SPELL N?

At the close of WWII, young NCOs selected for Officer Training were frequently given odd jobs to keep them occupied and to release someone else for more productive work, until they were called forward.

One such NCO was employed as a Company Orderly Corporal, working to a fearsome Sergeant Major of the Royal Ulster Rifles of prodigious valour in combat, as his Distinguished Conduct Medal proved, but of limited education. He had joined the Army in the thirties when the Recruiting Staff had not concerned themselves too closely with academic standards providing they filled their quota.

Writing out the daily company detail was more than a penance for the Sergeant Major. On one occasion he was struggling with the tasking of the three Platoons, which in this particular Company were lettered N, O and P, when the Company Orderly Corporal came in. 'Hey youse,' called the Sergeant Major, 'you're an educated f----r aren't you?' The Corporal admitted to having been to school. 'Well,' said the Sergeant Major, 'how d'youse spell N Platoon?' 'Just the letter N and the word Platoon,' replied the Corporal, completely nonplussed. 'Jeez,' said the Sergeant Major, 'I know there are two upright strokes but which way does the middle one go?'

One wonders how he would have fared in the post-war army.

ALWAYS COUNT YOUR CHICKENS CAREFULLY

The arrival in their Battalions of the first post-war output from Sandhurst was greeted with great acclaim by the old hands who had been waiting for the opportunity to off-load some of their less

3

attractive secondary jobs such as civil labour officer, officers' mess secretary, sanitation supervisory officer, to name but a few.

Thus it was that one very green Second Lieutenant, on joining his unit in Greece, found himself spending almost as much of his 'free' time as officers' mess secretary (read finance officer) as he did on military duty commanding his Platoon.

The main problem was the Mess Sergeant, who was, to all intents and purposes, the Mess Manager. The RAF have a specialised trade for mess staff with their own promotion structure, as do the Royal Navy, but the Army tend to push into their messes anyone who can be 'spared' from regimental duty. The Mess Sergeant at this particular time had no aptitude for running what was virtually a transit hotel for officers and was in the post solely because of an injury sustained to his back in an ambush in what was then called Palestine. This effectively precluded him from normal duty in a rifle company. The Mess Sergeant was not interested in book-keeping and at some stage he had made an error in his stocktaking which showed him to be several bottles of whisky and a dozen crates of beer surplus. Instead of double-checking the paperwork, he invited several of his Sergeants' Mess cronies, the MT Sergeant, the Cook Sergeant and various others, to polish off the lot (shades of Bilko – several decades before his time). The error recurred each month and every time the cronies assembled to absorb the surplus.

Nemesis caught up with this in the form of the Audit Board, which decided that the Mess Sergeant was liable for a bill of several hundreds of pounds. The up-shot was that he was busted to Corporal and transferred to HQ Company where, after many years as the Post Corporal, he was awarded the British Empire Medal for services over and above the call of duty. There must be a moral somewhere!

WHAT A WAY TO GET POSTED

The élite of the British Forces at that time were the British Military Mission to Greece (BMMG) tasked with rebuilding the Greek Armed Forces to combat the Communist Revolutionaries, who were attempting to take over the country. Not only did they live in the lap of luxury in Athens, with ready access to night life and staff cars, but they also received four bob a day mission pay for the 'hardships' they suffered. Not unnaturally, they were the envy of the British Infantry Battalions deployed operationally in the outback and who enjoyed none of these good things.

The Adjutant of one of the Battalions was an Infantry Captain who had had a hard war and, operational deployment or not, he was determined to enjoy himself and catch up – as he put it – on his lost youth.

This appeared to involve a shacking up with a different lady each night, which was fine until a routine Military Police check discovered him. The MP report read something like this:

'I am Cpl Smith of the Royal Military Police. On ? at around 2300hrs in company with LCpl Jones, I entered a house which I had reason to believe was being used for immoral purposes. I entered a room and found a man and a woman in bed unclothed. I asked him if he was a soldier and he replied, 'No, I am not a soldier – I am an officer.' I took down his particulars, verified these from his ID card, paid the compliments due to a commissioned officer and withdrew.'

The CO was not amused when he read the report and sacked the Adjutant on the spot. He was at once posted to the BMMG, promoted into a major's vacancy and granted the highly-prized mission pay on which he lived it up in Central Athens.

It was surprising how many other Captains took to visiting houses of ill repute in the hope of emulating this administrative sleight of hand – but a trick like that could only work once. Some people are just born lucky!

PERSPECTIVES DIFFER FROM WHEREVER YOU STAND

When 1 SUFFOLK moved from the Civil War in Greece to another type of war in Malaya in the late forties, the Advance Party were quartered for a few days in Nee Soon Transit Camp on Singapore Island while waiting to attend the Jungle Warfare course. This was a repository for all manner of military odds and sods in the Far East, one of whom was a Major Paymaster under close arrest for fiddling the funds and hence awaiting Court Martial. One of the officers in transit was always detailed as his escort (to make sure he didn't run away, perhaps. Where to? one is bound to ask).

He had apparently worked a racket on the exchange of Sterling to State Dollars when the troopships docked and got away with some £50,000; not an inconsiderable sum at late nineteen-forties prices.

The other Paymasters all thought of him as a local hero. 'He'll get five years but so what? When he comes out, he'll have all that lovely lolly in his coded account in Switzerland, at compound interest. Wish I'd thought of it!'

The hero had ample funds at his disposal and had a party in his room every night, to which all his Paymaster friends were invited. The unfortunate escort officer had to choose between staying stone cold sober or joining in. There weren't many escort officers who finished their stint in a sober state!

Ultimately the Paymaster did get five years – and was last heard of running an up-market hotel on the Riviera. Some people are natural survivors.

3

Malayan Emergency

1 SUFFOLK was dispatched from Greece to Malaya in early 1949, where they relieved 3rd GRENADIER GUARDS in Central Selangor. The Battalion joined a number of other British Infantry Battalions and virtually all the Gurkha Battalions, which had been transfered to the British Army when India became independent in 1947, on active operations against communist terrorists seeking to overthrow the rule of law and, ultimately, take over the country.

D Company 1 SUFFOLK was based in a former Chinese school at Kajang, a small town on the main Kuala Lumpur to Singapore road, which was bounded on one side by the jungle-covered hills of the main range, which bisected the Malayan peninsula from North to South, and on the other by the vast Kuala Langat block of jungle marked on the somewhat unreliable maps as 'unexplored – probably swamp'.

The Company Commander was a man of action who had fought the Japanese in Burma and regarded chasing communist terrorists as scarcely worthy of the term 'military operation'. Nonetheless, he quickly set about dominating that part of his operational area which bounded the rubber estates on either side of the main road and from whose numerous kampongs (villages), largely inhabited by rubber tappers, terrorists drew their principal support.

The first operation attempted was a small-scale ambush based on information from the Special Branch, which resulted in two dead terrorists. It might have been more had not the Special Branch guide become over-excited in the heat of the moment and rushed off in pursuit of the remainder, getting himself shot dead in the process by the flanking bren gun group which was unaware that he had left his assigned position. By the time the inevitable confusion was sorted out (of the ten soldiers involved only the Sergeant had ever been in action before) the three surviving terrorists were long gone – but a valuable lesson was learnt (or perhaps relearned) on the necessity for absolute control when in ambush positions, which paid dividends in later operations.

The Company Commander decided, rightly as it turned out, that the five terrorists engaged by the ambush party must form part of a larger group. He and his Platoon Commanders spent a tense evening poring over maps and trying to out think the local terrorist commander.

"Oh stop moaning, its the same for all of us."

Finally, it was decided that the terrorists were intending to raid and perhaps destroy the two European-run rubber estates surrounding the isolated village of Broga, high in the mountains at the end of a one-track road. Accordingly, the Company deployed at first light next morning (trying to move through jungle by night is not a productive activity) with one Platoon sweeping to the North and one to the South, with Company HQ controlling progress from the axis of the road. 10 Platoon, much to their chagrin, were left behind, partly to secure the base against attack and partly to provide a mobile reserve which could be moved (in vehicles) to blocking positions, if required. (This was in the days before helicopter mobility changed the face of minor tactics, although 'the' helicopter (was there really only one?) was occasionally used for VIP visits and evacuating casualties.)

During the day it transpired that the 'O' Group had guessed wrong. The terrorists hadn't gone on to Broga but had turned off, possibly as a result of the previous day's ambush, to attack the hydro-electric power station which supplied current to the local area. This was an unguarded facility – there just weren't enough troops to guard everything – and it was burnt to the ground following the murder of the duty crew of four Indian power workers.

This news reached the Company Base from the Malayan Police in the late morning and the Commander of 10 Platoon, having failed to make contact with the rest of the Company on the radio, since both the extreme range and the atmospheric conditions for High Frequency transmission at midday in the tropics were against him, decided to take a Patrol to make physical contact with the Company HQ near Broga. Leaving his Sergeant to guard the base with the bulk of the Platoon, he set off with six men in two jeeps along a short cut up a former logging track, which was just passable for some miles by agile vehicles with four-wheeled drive. When the track ran out, the vehicles were concealed and the radio operator and the two drivers were left to guard them, while the other four set off across a jungle ridge to where it was fondly expected they would soon be able to locate Company HQ. Just over the crest of the ridge was an old logging camp, long abandoned by the forestry workers, and there, much to their surprise, the little group came upon the terrorist gang, clearly taking a rest after distancing themselves from the power station they had destroyed early that morning.

There was no way of determining how many terrorists there were at the time, although intelligence later set it at around thirty. The Platoon Commander and his three men were virtually on top of the camp before they realised quite what they had blundered into and happily, having their weapons ready, were able to get off the first shots which killed two of the terrorists. (At this point the Platoon Commander's sten gun – a notoriously unreliable weapon – jammed with an empty case in the chamber. His instructor at the

9

Small Arms School would have been proud of the speed with which immediate action drill was carried out to clear the stoppage.) Meantime, in view of the disparity in numbers, an element of bluff was called for and the Platoon Commander started exhorting B Company to 'get up on the right flank' and C Company on the left at the top of his not inconsiderable lungs.

Having lost another man, the terrorists leader (so it was assumed as he had risen from a long-discarded deck chair when the action started) decided to call it a day and gave some command in Chinese, at which the terrorists literally melted into the jungle. The Platoon Commander decided not to chance his luck much further and having secured the weapons of the three dead terrorists, returned to the rest of his group by the jeeps, where by some fluke of weather conditions, the radio operator had made contact with the rest of the Company. Unhappily, they were too far from the contact to do more than send out follow-up patrols which later accounted for another terrorist who had been so badly wounded as to be unable to keep up with his comrades.

THIS ALL CAME AS A BIT OF A SHOCK COS I THOUGHT KUALA LUMPUR WAS NORTH OF WREXHAM.

Nonetheless, the purely chance contact with the terrorists so soon after their attack on the power station established a degree of moral ascendancy by D Company, which the Company Commander took considerable pains to maintain. The overall effect was to make the terrorists more cautious, more suspicious of informers and to base themselves deeper in the jungle.

Paradoxically, this was of some assistance to the company as the track of a substantial group in virgin jungle is much easier to follow than in the confusion of paths in and around the jungle edge.

The Platoon Commander and his team of three came to realise later that they had been pretty lucky to see off several times their own number in their first contact of the campaign – but they did what they had been trained to do – engage the enemy – and made use of a simple deception to disguise their lack of strength. 'Who dares wins?' – Well it worked on this occasion.

★

One of the odder mysteries of human nature is how people react to the stress of combat. Corporal Pancote was viewed by all as a white hope, a dead cert to make RSM and possibly commissioned rank later. He was always smart, efficient, a brilliant instructor and popular with everyone.

Come the time of the first taste of hand – to – hand combat, while other patrols were closing with the enemy, Corporal Pancote was down behind the largest tree he could find exhorting his soldiers to take cover and conserve their ammunition.

Private Powsett, on the other hand, was the biggest and scruffiest rogue in the Battalion, likeable perhaps but always in trouble of one sort or another. In the same action it was quickly learnt that there was another side to Powsett. He was up there with a sub machine gun he'd picked up from a casualty and giving the enemy absolute stick with grenades as well as bullets, which encouraged his colleagues to greater efforts.

After this Corporal Pancote was quickly dispatched to the Malay Local Forces Training Centre in Singapore where he was immediately promoted Sergeant, while Private Powsett remained the rough and ready soldier he had always been, albeit with a Military Medal up. Justice is not always poetic.

The whole operation was wrong footed from the start. It got off the mark almost an hour late due to transport problems, the route in had to be changed and all the carefully planned rehearsals went straight up the spout. Familiar story? You bet it is – to anyone who has been involved in Internal Security Operations. Let's start from the beginning.

The counter terrorist campaign in Malaya in the early fifties threw up some incredible characters, one of whom was a Mr Pagden, who had become almost a legend in Force 136 operating against the Japs in southern Malaya in WWII. He had gravitated to Special Branch when the Malayan emergency started and ran a motley collection of cut throats, mostly surrendered or captured terrorists, known in the trade as Pag's people.

South of Kuala Lumpur, on the Kajang Road, was a squatter area known as Belakong. While this was effectively a suburb of the capital, it was just inside the Kajang District geographically and nothing – but nothing – is more inflexible than local authority boundaries. Hence urban Kuala Lumpur Police wouldn't touch it and the Kajang Police, with bigger fish to fry in the deep jungles further south, felt that Belakong just wasn't their problem. Into this no-man's land came an intelligent and highly dangerous terrorist leader called Yap Yong, who had also operated with great success against the Japanese. He regarded himself as a latter-day Robin Hood and was careful only to put the financial squeeze on the prosperous Chinese of the capital itself.

He was immensely popular in Belakong and while, as local commissar, he controlled a group of 40 odd well armed terrorists, he and his two bodyguards were wont to operate quite openly on Mao's 'fish in the sea' principle among the local population, with a highly developed early warning network of supporters to give notice of the approach of the Security Forces. (Shades of the Ballymurphy dustbin lids, still over two decades into the future.)

He was high on the Wanted List and many ambushes had been laid and other operations launched against his group but somehow he had always managed to escape often passing a Yah Boo message to the Security Forces after each failure. But Yap Yong had a weakness; women! He developed quite a style in 'putting it about'

12

among the nubile nymphs of Belakong, which in some strange way enhanced his reputation. Not unnaturally, his wife, who lived a nominally respectable life as a laundress, didn't take kindly to all these extramural activities. All this was reported to Mr Pagden, who lined up one of the more persuasive of his band of thugs, known as Ticus (the mouse) because of his small stature and long nose, and told him to get close to this lady. This ploy was more successful than even Mr Pagden thought possible and by the 'let me take you away from all this' concept, the lady was induced to 'shop' her husband and his immediate henchmen, effectively becoming an early version of the supergrass. A plan was developed to identify the hut, one out of several hundreds, which Yap Yong was using as a temporary safe house, when he and his team returned from their nightly collection of enforced taxes from the Chinese community in the city, plus perhaps a murder or two to discourage any ideas of co-operating with the authorities. A cordon would be thrown around the hut and that, hopefully, would be the end of Yap Yong. The lady, her new boyfriend and two other former terrorists were to lead a Platoon of 1 SUFFOLK by circuitous route to approach the area from an unexpected direction so as not to alert the network of 'watchers'. This all depended on the use of a civilian truck to approach Belakong, the distinctive whine of the Army 3 tonner being a certain give away.

The Battalion Intelligence Officer, who had set up the operation with Mr Pagden, had arranged a civilian truck with the local Special Branch Sub Inspector, but, sadly, his colloquial Malay wasn't as good as he thought it was and the truck turned up at seven in the morning instead of seven at night.

After wasting some 30 minutes, by which time it was dark, it was obvious that the plan would have to be drastically altered. A four-way discussion then ensued in English, Malay, Hokkien and Cantonese, since the four Chinese spoke two different dialects, which determined that (a) this operation could not be postponed since the lady would be missed and the whole thing aborted and (b) because of the delay and having to use an army truck, only a 'crash action' had any chance of success.

It was impossible to work out where the objective was from the lady's description, which suffered from having to be translated twice, but it became apparent that it was close to the jungle edge

13

and only a few hundred metres from the road. It was decided that the lady and her escorts would lead the Platoon to the hut while the Intelligence Officer, who had come along for the ride, would set up a firm base on the jungle edge to act as a support group, RV, reserve or whatever, depending on how the situation developed. This wasn't exactly a strong force, comprising merely the Platoon HQ Bren Group and the Flame Thrower Team consisting of the Battalion's APTC Sergeant Instructor who operated the Ackpack itself, with the Sports Storeman as his escort. The use of Flame was not unusual for short range operations at this time. Not only was it both effective and terrifying (to the enemy) but it was also more selective than small arms fire in a squatter area, teeming with people, when any number of non-participants were liable to get clobbered by the 'overs'.

There was no time for refinements. The Platoon debussed and went in at the double in the darkness through the squatter area, with every form of alarm being given by the locals, while the support group peeled off to the jungle edge.

Despite the early warning system, a degree of surprise was achieved and the Platoon Sergeant, leading a group to the rear of the hut indicated by the lady, came face to face with the more villainous of Yap Young's henchmen who was attempting to leave through a window opening. He fired at the approaching troops, missed, and was cut down by a short burst from the Sergeant's Owen gun.

The Platoon Commander led an assualt group into the hut in the finest School of Infantry FIBUA tradition to find only a dead Chinese of great antiquity drilled neatly through the skull by a stray shot from the Platoon Sergeant's burst (it transpired later that he was the co-ordinator of the early warning systems). While there was no sign of Yap Yong, there were enormous quantities of documents visible with probably others and maybe weapons too hidden in and around the hut. The Platoon went into all-round defence and the Commander conferred briefly with the Intelligence Officer on his primitive but effective 88 set. They agreed to stay put until first light, a sensible precaution in a hostile area in pitch darkness when the geography was unfamiliar. Nonetheless, it was decided to lay an ambush on the main track leading into the jungle to deal with any of Yap Young's troops who might choose to investigate the earlier shooting and hopefully to scoop up Yap Yong himself who was clearly still at large somewhere in the squatter area and might attempt to break out to join his main group.

Fortunately, Ticus knew the lie of the land, having visited the area during his courtship of the lady, and was able to lead the ambush party into position. After a quick briefing the group set off passing within earshot of the support group. As the sound of their passing died away, a new sound became apparent emanating from a small rice paddy from which some peasant sought to supplement his income. It resolved itself into two people moving carefully out of the water in the wake of the ambush group taking advantage of the noise they were making to hide their own.

Most of the support group were masked from this movement by a patch of scrub but the PT Sergeant was not. Appreciating that the two figures emerging from the rice paddy must be Yap Yong and his remaining henchman, he hosed them both down with a wet shot from his flame thrower and then lit them both up with a live jet. The effect was dramatic. They took fire at once and tried to dive back into the rice paddy, with the Sports Storeman banging away at them with his rifle. The Bren Group finally got into the act with a series of short bursts and the Intelligence Officer did his best with his M1 carbine. The two Chinese with the main body also joined in with great enthusiasm but minimal accuracy, one shooting the other in the shoulder in his excitement (fortunately not seriously), while the ambush group, reversing course, also opened up but with a higher degree of control and considerably greater accuracy. Never had two terrorists picked up a greater weight of lead; they were very very dead, quite apart from being fried.

The search of the area in daylight produced even more documents which together with supplementary information from the lady, enabled Special Branch to progressively eliminate a number of the most active communist cells in the south of the city, while their very effective psyops department (it was still called white propaganda at the time) had a field day debunking the Yap Yong legend. True to Mr Pagden's promise, Ticus was transferred, with the lady, to Penang and perhaps they lived happily ever after.

15

So an operation which started badly ended as a considerable success – lucky, some might say, but it's surprising how often luck comes to those with the initiative to seize an opportunity and the flexibility to make quick changes to a plan.

Who shot Yap Yong? Practically every participant on the operation thought they had but did it matter? The real gain was that his demise formed a turning point and virtually ended the power of the communists in Belakong.

PERSISTENCE AND PATIENCE CAN PAY OFF

The protracted campaign in Malaya against the Communist Terrorists was going well by the early fifties and the enemy had been forced to retreat deeper into the jungle in order to survive. The corollary to this was that the Security Forces had to patrol further and further into the remote areas to seek and destroy the terrorists.

When there was no positive information on the whereabouts of the enemy, the technique used in 1 SUFFOLK was to deploy platoon-sized patrols to suspicious areas for a fourteen-day cycle, a time-scale which was effectively limited by the quantity of rations which could be carried.

10 Platoon had spent a fortnight searching a sector of the Kuala Langat jungle swamp without picking up as much as a sniff of the enemy. They were heartily sick of compo rations and being wet through, since the water level varied from knee deep to shoulder high depending on the contours of the jungle floor and the degree of rainfall in the mountains during the previous few days. The Platoon Commander made what he believed would be his final radio call to his Company Base at seven in the morning before setting course for a link up on the nearest road. (It was standard practice to make radio contact at dawn and dusk daily when the atmospheric conditions for High Frequency propagation were optimal.) The Company Commander came on the air in person and explained that a group of terrorists had attacked a rubber estate which bordered the swamp during the previous night, burnt down the smoke house, murdered the Indian manager and his family and thoroughly intimidated the resident Chinese rubber

16

tappers. The Malayan Police thought the enemy had turned South but it was just possible that some had turned North towards the area where the Platoon was operating.

10 Platoon were to remain in the jungle for a further 48 hours and patrol the edge of the swamp, try and pick up the trail of any terrorists seeking refuge therein and destroy them. These crystal clear orders were not greeted with any great enthusiasm by 10 Platoon particularly since they had run out of tea and the thought of living for two more days on 'neat' swamp water, albeit sterilised (which only made it taste worse) and their emergency rations – singularly unappetizing blocks of concentrate known colloquially as snake's s--t – did not appeal one little bit.

Nonetheless, 'orders is orders' and the Platoon struck out for the edge of the jungle swamp which they reached around mid-day. The Platoon Commander sent one Section to check the jungle edge to the North, giving them a RV for the following afternoon, while he led the rest of the Platoon South towards the area of the terrorists' recent atrocity.

Several false tracks were followed into the jungle swamp, all of which turned out to be either the track of wild pig, which flourished in the area, or old tracks, some perhaps made by the security forces on previous patrols. It was getting dark and raining with that type of downpour only found in the tropics when a faint track was picked up, recent enough but probably yet another wild pig. The Platoon Commander decided to have one last go before going into all-round defence for the night. He led the Platoon cautiously into the swamp, following the track with difficulty in the fading light but helped by the noise of the rain on the foliage, which effectively drowned the noise of their progress. After several hundred metres, a fragment of a 'Good Morning' towel of the type favoured by the terrorists as sweat rags, was found on a thorn bush. This relatively insignificant sign indicated the likely presence of the enemy and was passed down the line by silent signal, so essential in jungle warfare. A contact was coming. The Platoon began to perk up – maybe they weren't wasting their time. Safety catches were eased off and magazines were given an extra push to make sure they were fully home.

A few metres further on, the Platoon Commander became aware of an atap basha almost invisible in the gloom, from which

17

there emerged at that moment a single terrorist with a sub-machine gun in one hand and a cooking pot in the other. He never lived to enjoy whatever he proposed to cook. The Platoon Commander's carbine cut him down with a single burst. The rest of the Platoon deployed to the right and left, a procedure they practised constantly, and engaged the other terrorists in the basha. The result was something of an anti-climax. There were only two more, albeit they were rich in lead, a tribute to the accuracy of the Platoon's fire in the prevailing deluge and the failing light.

Having deployed the Platoon round the shelter, another standard procedure, the Platoon Commander and one of his Corporals carried out a rapid search of the area. Although only three terrorists had been killed, there were the packs of a further three, indicating that they were away on some mission and clearly intended to return. The chance of an ambush was too good to miss but since it was now pitch dark there was no opportunity for refinements. The Platoon Commander, a Corporal, and two soldiers hid the dead terrorists in a thicket and concealed themselves in the basha as best they could while the Platoon Sergeant led the rest a couple of hundred metres deeper into the swamp, where they could be out of sight and sound even in daylight but readily available as a reserve, and deployed them in pairs in a broad semi circle, centred on the basha.

It was almost impossible to doze, let alone sleep, in these conditions but the British soldier can sleep on the proverbial clothes line and one member of each pair was soon far away with the other watchful and ready, prodding his partner forcibly in the ribs if he managed even a light snore. In the basha itself, it was even more tense with three facing towards the track by which it was expected the enemy would approach, while the fourth covered the flanks and rear. After a long wait of almost eight hours, punctuated by surreptitious slaps as the Platoon tried to drive off the resident swarm of mosquitoes who were feasting on this unexpected bonus to their diet, the sounds of a stealthy approach became apparent. Although it had stopped raining the thickness of the overhead jungle canopy effectively cut out even a glimmer of light.

After a few minutes, it was clear that the remaining terrorists were returning, since they stopped short and called softly in Chinese, obviously giving some sort of password. The ambush group kept silent, hoping the newcomers would believe that their comrades were all fast asleep and would come on in. After an agonising pause, this they duly did.

In the darkness, the Platoon Commander let the leading terrorist get so close that he could actually touch the bridge of his nose with the muzzle of his carbine. A short burst opened the action which took off the top of the terrorist's head. His two henchmen opened up on the remainder winging one with their crossfire, who dropped into the swamp groaning. The third, who was further back, made a detour past the basha and headed for the deeper jungle where, fortunately, he ran slap into one of the pairs deployed by the Platoon Sergeant. 'Shoot anything that moves,' the Sergeant had said – so they did! – result – one dead terrorist.

It was still two hours to first light and in accordance with their rigid rule of not moving at night, the Platoon stuck it out with only the groans of the wounded terrorist to indicate that anything had happened at all. Came the dawn, the latest three terrorists were recovered, the injured man having died of his wounds, and radio contact made with the Company Base for transport and a carrying party (deceased terrorists had to be recovered for identification by Special Branch from their extensive 'wanted lists').

The sequel followed from detailed examination of the documents found on the dead terrorists and their impedimentia at which the Malayan Police Special Branch excelled. The Chinese have a bad habit (for them) of keeping extensive records of all sorts of transactions and from these a number of terrorist supporters, leading nominally respectable lives in the settled areas, were identified and arrested. This led to further information and in the snowball effect of all this a whole kampong of communist sympathisers was resettled in a 'new village' where they could be kept under proper surveillance.

And the Platoon? As a reward for their efforts, instead of the usual 48 hour break between patrols, they were allowed a week at the rest camp by the sea at Port Dickson to unwind and get the swamp out of their system. They had been lucky – yes – but they were carefully and continuously trained for their task and it's surprising how often luck comes the way of those with the imagination and energy to seize it.

(As an aside, this all took place in the days of National Service –

10 platoon was almost entirely composed of young men doing their two years' compulsory service – and very good soldiers they proved. The motivation common to both regular and national servicemen alike was to stay alive. It must have been more difficult to motivate National Servicemen in the UK and in Germany, where the threat to their survival was less obvious.)

THE 'THING' THAT SHOT HIS COMMANDING OFFICER

1 SUFFOLK had just completed a long blanket ambush operation and several Platoons were given 48 hours R and R. The Platoon Commanders decided to take their break in the capital, Kuala Lumpur, only half an hour away, and all piled into a Scout car which was heading that way to escort a vehicle collecting a new draft from England. As they were leaving, the Adjutant stopped them and asked them to meet and brief a new 'thing', as baby second lieutenants were termed at that time, and send him on to Battalion Headquarters.

The train from Singapore was delayed having been shot up, as was not unusual, on its way through Johore and by the time it finally arrived disgorging a pale and shaken 'thing' – all white knees and baggy shorts – the assembled Platoon Commanders had, as they say, drink taken.

They greeted the 'thing' effusively and proceeded to instruct him on how to operate the twin machine guns on the Scout car, making out that he was highly likely to be ambushed on his way up to the Battalion. Someone asked his name, only to be told by some-one else that the 'thing' was sure to be killed that afternoon, so why bother. The route was in fact probably the safest in the whole of Malaya but the 'thing' dutifully went off in the Scout car, avidly training his machine guns on every passing piece of scrub, while the Platoon Commanders proceeded to their delayed debauch.

On arrival (safely, of course) in the Battalion Base Camp, the 'thing' went through the drill he had learnt at Sandhurst to clear the machine guns – but, in his highly nervous state, he made one mistake; he forgot to take off the magazines before squeezing the triggers. The early evening quiet of the Base Camp was rent by the sound of two long bursts of tracer which, from the purely random

20

angle of barrels, was pointing straight at the one Nissen hut which housed the CO's office, passing in through the window and out through the wall at the back. The Adjutant rushed in to find the CO in the knee hole of his desk, with a pistol in both hands, thinking he was about to be assassinated. 'Is the enemy attacking?' he asked. 'No Sir,' replied the Adjutant, 'I think it was the new "thing" arriving.' The 'thing' was duly extracted from the Scout car and dragged before a furious Commanding Officer, who was unused to being shot at by his own Officers. 'I'll put you in front of the Brigadier,' he stated flatly. 'You'll probably lose a year's seniority – and since you've only been a second lieutenant for four weeks, that will make you minus eleven months; which on your present performance is about your mark!'

The Brigadier in question had, by some fluke of fate, decided that week to visit one of the most remote Company Bases in the Selangor Swamps, accessible only along a track prone to constant ambush, and perforce had to travel in a Scout car.

The Scout car duly reported to his Command Post but a Staff Officer indicated that the Brigadier's visit would have to be postponed since the gunner had gone sick. 'I'll work the guns myself,' said the Brigadier, climbing aboard and placing two 50 round drum magazines on the machine guns. What he did next is obscure but two long bursts of tracer went whistling round the Brigade Headquarters, with passing soldiers, contractors, staff officers and assorted hangers-on all diving for the nearest cover. The RSM came running out, 'Who fired those f-----g guns?' he shouted. 'The Brigadier,' said someone. 'Well shot, Sir,'said the RSM, coming stiffly to the salute. The Armourer Sergeant, swiftly summoned, pronounced that the sears were worn (and was promoted to Staff Sergeant the next day – coincidence perhaps!) and the Brigadier's visit proceeded.

When the unfortunate 'thing' was marched in front of the Brigadier a few days later, he found not a fierce but almost a father figure confronting him. 'You've been a very careless thing,' said the Brigadier, 'and you might have killed your Commanding Officer – but I know just how easy it is for these unfortunate things to happen. I could tell you a similar story . . . No, it's too painful. Now go away and be a good thing in the future and we'll say no more about it.'

The CO was livid but the 'thing' went on to earn rank and distinction. As he once said in later life, after such a start, things could only get better. Amen to that.

DOING THINGS TOGETHER CAN BE CARRIED TOO FAR

During the Malayan emergency, the night train from Singapore to Kuala Lumpur was regularly shot up as it wound its way through the tangle of jungle-covered foothills of North Johore. D Company 1 SUFFOLK was tasked to prevent this and used the Company's two Ackpack Flamethrowers to good effect on the most obvious positions, which reduced the secondary jungle to a barren heap of ashes, at least for a few weeks.

As a result, the terrorists took to sniping at the train, the easiest of targets, from further into the jungle and well beyond the limited range of the flamethrower, so some other means of suppression was necessary. D Company devised a simple plan for four soldiers, each armed with a bren gun and a box of twelve magazines, loaded alternately with one ball and one tracer, to board the night train at Bekok, its first stop in their sector, and to put down 'prophylactic fire' (as it was called) on likely terrorist firing areas as far as Segamat, the provincial capital. Four bren guns firing rapid can put down quite a weight of fire and the incidence of sniping at the train decreased dramatically.

On one steamy night at the height of the rains, a Platoon Commander and three soldiers boarded the train at Bekok for the nightly firework display with their bren guns. Sadly, they failed to appreciate that among the train's passengers was a draft of Gurkhas, fresh from their training depot in Nepal, en route to their Battalion, far up country in Pahang. They had each been issued with a rifle and 50 rounds in Singapore and given some rudimentary instruction about firing back if the train was ambushed. When they heard the D Company bren gunners doing their thing, being the natural warriors that they were, they immediately got into the act by lowering their compartment windows and discharging their pieces into the jungle with more enthusiasm than accuracy. This was fine while the night train made its tortuous way through the jungle-covered hills but not so appropriate when it wound through the sparce suburbs of Segamat and finally stopped at the station.

The D Company group had stopped firing long before but would the Gurkhas? Would they, hell. The Platoon Commander and his group did the best they could but having no Gurkhali and the Gurkhas having no English it was at best a somewhat limited interchange. Finally, it dawned on the Gurkhas that, good sport though it might be, it was not entirely appropriate to be firing through the windows of a station waiting room, where the would-be passengers had sensibly prostrated themselves on the floor as the train approached, having heard the fusillade from afar.

The only person to come out of the incident with any credit was the Indian Station Master, who acquired a white flag from somewhere and approached the train waving his flag and screaming for the firing to stop. When it did, his station looked distinctly the worse for wear and required extensive repair by the Public Works Dept, although by some miracle no one was injured.

What became known as the Slaughter of Segamat passed into legend but subsequently drafts of Gurkhas were more carefully briefed. It could have been a disaster, and what a propaganda field day the terrorists would have had if several innocent bystanders had been killed. Perhaps the sun really does shine on the righteous!

COs ARE TRAINED TO EXERCISE DISCRETION

On one occasion, circa 1950, a Platoon of D Company were closing in on a terrorist camp in the Kuala Langat swamps of South Selangor, having followed up a group of terrorists from a raid they had perpetrated on a local Kampong (Malay village). On approaching the terrorist hideout, the Platoon split into two assault groups, one led by the Platoon Commander and the other by the Platoon Sergeant, as was the Standard Operating Procedure at that time, so as to invest the enemy from two directions simultaneously.

The Platoon Sergeant's Group had the worst approach through a deeper part of the swamp and the Sergeant, in the lead, had just crossed a fallen log, with difficulty, since he was shoulder deep in water, when he was fired on by an enemy sentry. Happily, the bullet went slightly high and passed through the Sergeant's floppy jungle hat only to hit the second man, carrying a bren machine gun, who was at that instant crossing the fallen log. It caught him right on the lower abdomen and the scream that rent the jungle could be heard from many miles, the genitals being a sensitive part of the anatomy to take a bullet.

The Platoon had its little battle, fortunately without further casualties to themselves, and then radioed for help for the wounded man. This was in the early days of rotary wing aircraft and 'the' helicopter was dispatched (there was only one!) to recover him to hospital. The Platoon sweated blood cutting a clearing for the chopper to land and eventually the casualty was whipped off to the Military Hospital.

Some weeks later, the Platoon Commander, who had been wounded in another action and was not yet fit to return to the jungle, was standing in for the Adjutant who was on leave. During this time, the casualty from the swamp attack was arrested by the Royal Military Police for being in an 'out-of-bounds' area of Kuala Lumpur. Normally the Acting Adjutant would have dealt with the affair quickly and quietly but the regulations were quite clear that a RMP charge could only be heard before the Commanding Officer personally. The Acting Adjutant arranged a hearing and the RMP NCO stated in the mechanical dalek-like voice of his calling, 'I was investigating premises which were suspected of being used for immoral purposes. I entered a room and found a man and a woman in bed, unclothed. I took down his particulars and now identify him as being Private Still of 1st Bn The Suffolk Regiment, whom I now recognise . . . etc., etc.'

The Commanding Officer heard all the evidence and got to the point where he had to ask the accused if he had anything to say. 'Well Sir,' said Private Still, 'you know as how I had one of my goolies shot off in the South Swamp?' The Commanding Officer agreed that he was aware of Private Still's unfortunate disability. 'Well Sir,' he went on, 'I wanted to see if it still worked.' The Commanding Officer couldn't resist asking, 'Well Still, did it work?' 'Yes Sir,' replied Still, grinning from ear to ear. 'Worked like a charm.' 'Case Dismissed. March Out!'

4

Interlude in England

A FRIGHTENING EXPERIENCE

Many moons ago, when she was recovering from an unfortunate romantic experience, a member of a noble family was appointed Colonel in Chief of a County Regiment.

Arrangements were made for her to visit the Depot of the Regiment at Bury St Edmunds, en route for another engagement in East Anglia. A young Captain commanding the Training Company was detailed to organise a Guard of Honour of two officers and ninety-six from his company and various hangers on lurking in the Depot awaiting posting. The Guard practised many times during the weeks leading up to the VIP visit and by the Sunday of the ceremony they thought themselves as perfect as they were ever likely to be.

The Guard was drawn up on the Square with the Captain on its flank, standing on his 'spot'; a large white cross painted on the tarmac. The Noble Lady was supposed to stop on a similar white cross to receive his compliments before inspecting the Guard. Sadly, her Assistant had travelled in another car which had broken down en route with the result that no one had explained exactly to the Lady where she was supposed to stop and, in the event, she overshot her cross by upwards of a metre. The Captain, overcome by the splendour of the occasion, failed to appreciate how close she was when his sword descended in the graceful arc of the traditional salute, the point caught her left breast. None was sure who was most surprised by the turn of events, the Noble Lady or the Captain.

Meanwhile, his fellow officers in the crowd, who had observed the incident through their binoculars, had begun to lay their bets – 'That's Joe finished. Will he be shot or put in the Tower?' or 'Wonder who'll get command of his Company?' – and also, for the more discerning, 'She is a Noble Lady after all – is it red blood or blue?'

But the Lady had an enormous reserve of sang-froid. Despite the tear in the front of her dress she inspected the Guard without batting an eyelid. Admittedly, immediately thereafter she shot into the ladies loo at the double where her Assistant produced a repair kit from her pants (or whatever) and cobbled it all together.

The Captain discovered later that the point of his sword had only torn the noble dress and perhaps even the noble bra (although this remained a grey area!). Happily, it had not touched the Noble Person, which probably explains why he was never Court Martialled and served to become a Brigadier.

KEN YE NO UNDERSTAND GUID SCOSS

During the fifties, the Army Staff College carried out a Battlefield Tour of the Normandy landings and the subsequent campaign to capture Caen (which inevitably became corrupted to the Bottlefield Tour, in view of the easy access to the local vino). The Course travelled by Dakotas, which were still flying at the time, and were somewhat put off when, having flown for some half an

26

hour over Normandy without landing, the co-pilot came from back the flight deck to ask if anyone could read a map. The local airfield, a grass strip, was not easy to find!

The speakers on the tour were all commanders who had participated in actual battles and were able to give a first-hand account of the stress of combat and the problems they had faced.

One early morning, the Course visited the scene of the breakout across the swamps of the River Dives by 8 PARA and were privileged to be addressed by the officer who was in command during the battle, an Airborne Warrior of enormous distinction with a DSO and no less than three Bars, as well as an MC and various foreign awards for gallantry.

This officer hailed from Dunbartonshire, where they speak a language barely known to man, and his wartime exploits had done nothing to improve his patois. He stood before the staff college students, all eager to learn from one of such experience, red of face and breathing heavily, having clearly 'drink taken' with his French colleagues on the previous evening. He was introduced by the Commandant and launched forth in his voluble Scots, which sounded remarkably like 'Auch Jock, therr wi' th' radge the noo f---ing Germans, an whoo hud tae gie 'em the crust f---ing Germans th' Jocks auch uck grr noo dinnae gut och f---ing Germans . . .' and so it went on for fifteen minutes with only two recognisable words in Anglo-Saxon popping up at intervals. A Canadian student asked a British Officer standing next to him for a translation. 'Search me,' he replied, 'all I could get of it was that he's not keen on the Germans.'

Some years later, one of the students, now commanding a Parachute Battalion, sought the great man's help over a presentation on the techniques of night attack, a subject in which he was acknowledged as the greatest living expert, and which was currently being re-examined having been out of favour for some years.

He was told he had an hour and a half to expand his theories. 'Rubbish,' said the great man, 'Ah dinnae wunt muir than a minnut and a half.'

When the day of the presentation came, it was duly billed for 1½ hours. The wily old Airborne Warrior rose to his feet and announced (in quite intelligible English), 'Night Attack. Ye get a thousand yards of white tape. Ye put a man every yard. I get the front end and say Follow Me,' – and sat down (in slightly less than a minute and a half). Simple – perhaps over simple – BUT IT WORKED. How else would he have been awarded the DSO for four separate actions. All those present learnt the lesson. The simple way is often most likely to succeed!

"Aaaagh you've caught my tie — "

"You are an 'orrible little man!
What are you?"

LEARNING THEIR NAMES MAKES PEOPLE FEEL WANTED

In the fifties, the Commandant of the Army Staff College at Camberley, a distinguished General with a brilliant war record as a Commander of Airborne Forces, had substantial power over the Directing Staff (DS). The DS at that time were all Majors, acting Lieutenant Colonel, and a good Confidential Report from the Commandant was a sure passport to having their acting Rank confirmed as substantive. They acted as instructors to the several Syndicates, each comprising ten young Captains aspiring to the magic letters psc (in the lower case) after their names, which would assure them of future promotion and a secure career in the service.

It was the Commandant's habit during the early weeks of the course to drop in on each Syndicate and sit quietly at the back for as long as 20 minutes, during which time the DS, thinking of his future prospects, gave his all to the subject under study. Not a bit of it. The Commandant really wasn't interested in the subject matter. He had a thing about learning the names of all the 150 student officers and spent his time in the Syndicate Rooms methodically memorising each one. He had, he said, discovered at an early age that soldiers were more inclined to do as you bid them if you were able to address them by their name and he felt the same should apply to officer students at Camberley.

It was something of a party piece of his, at the first Dining In Night of the Course, to take round some VIP colleague and introduce all his students by their name and regiment; no mean achievement.

He was doing his thing with one group of a dozen or so and identified one student as Sparrow, which brought a muffled mutter from the assembled officers. Realising that perhaps for once he hadn't got it entirely right he paused and said to the person concerned, 'It is Sparrow, isn't it?' 'No,' came the reply, 'Starling, Sir.'

Thereafter this became a source of constant amusement to the Commandant. Whenever he met this particular officer, perhaps in a corridor or on an exercise, he would prod him in the stomach with his cane and mutter 'Sparrow-Starling. Starling-Sparrow' and burst into gales of laughter.

The word quickly flashed around the DS. 'Don't monkey with Starling,' they said to each other. 'He and the Commandant are always laughing together over some joke or other. Vent your spleen on someone more vulnerable.'

It is possible to succeed at the Staff College without really trying, if you happen to be blessed with a slightly unusual name.

ALWAYS CHOOSE A TARGET WHICH CAN'T SHOOT BACK

The Deputy Commander of 158 Infantry Brigade (TA) was a full Colonel with a distinguished war record who, in civilian life, was the senior partner in a large firm of Solicitors in Birmingham. Before being promoted Colonel, he had commanded a TA

Battalion in South Staffordshire, again with considerable distinction, and, in the way these things have a habit of doing, problems from his previous appointment finally caught up with him.

In the fifties, the rates of pay on offer to the civilian staff of the TA units was so poor, in comparison to the wages available in manufacturing industry, that it was normal to enlist the Chief Clerk and his team into the TA as NCOs and to give them a substantial number of TA days' pay each month to supplement their meagre income, thus producing a living wage.

This was fine as far as it went, but someone overdid it in the South Staffordshires and gave the clerical staff 32 days' pay in a 31 day month. Eventually, this was picked up at the Regimental Pay Office audit and an investigation was initiated. This revealed not only that the practice was widespread, but also that the total sum involved over the years, ran into several thousand pounds. Since the CO is ultimately responsible for everything which happens in his unit, the Colonel thus received a bill for something in the order of £8,000. Having given himself legal advice, wearing his Solicitor's hat, he declined to pay and, after further machinations of bureaucracy, was deemed to have incurred 'the severe displeasure of the Army Council', which the local General was told to promulgate.

The General's staff rang the Colonel in his office 'You are to appear at the General's office in Shrewsbury at 0900 hrs on Monday morning to receive the severe displeasure of the Army Council,' he was told. 'Sorry,' replied the Colonel, 'in civilian life I am a Solicitor in a very busy practice and Monday is a working day. However, if the General would care to come to my office in Birmingham at 0900 hrs on Monday morning, I would be more than happy to receive from him the severe displeasure of the Army Council.'

At this point the military establishment gave up and sent it to him by post. He received a well-deserved CBE in the next Honours list and later hung in his loo both his CBE citation and his 'severe displeasure' letter just to prove – as he said – that action and reaction usually balance each other out.

5

Middle East Medley

BEWARE OF SWIMMING SOLDIERS

1 PARA was based in Bahrein in the sixties against the possibility of an incursion by Iraq against Kuwait, which was then considered by Her Majesty's Government to be at least a likely option. One Company was based at the RAF airfield as a 'fire brigade' on 4 hours notice, while the rest of the Battalion lived on a squalid patch of wind-swept desert which the soldiers christened 'the Alamo'. Not unnaturally, the four-week tour of duty at the airfield was regarded as a cushy number with its air conditioned barracks, swimming pool, large NAAFI and full programme of evening entertainment.

The RAF were commanded by a distinguished Group Captain who had started his service life in the Brigade of Guards and was determined to make his Station observe what he regarded as 'proper standards'. Amongst other things, this involved the RAF Duty Officer wearing full Service Dress with sword and medals; not much fun in the heat of the Gulf summer.

D Company 1 PARA had just returned from a long deployment in the Trucial States and, to their delight, took their turn as the Standby Force at the airfield. Several Toms, having had a relaxing few hours in the NAAFI, decided to try the pool and have a midnight swim. This did not accord with the RAF Standing Orders which forbade swimming after dark on the sensible premise that the swimmer would be vulnerable to mosquitoes which tended to operate nocturnally.

It was probably to be expected that the half dozen or so midnight bathers would be approached by the RAF Duty Officer, in full fig, and told to leave the pool at once. 'Sorry Sir,' said one of the Toms, 'water in my ears. Can't hear a word.' The RAF Officer advanced a few paces and repeated his demand. 'Sorry Sir,' said the Tom, 'I really can't hear a thing. Could you come a bit closer?'

31

The RAF Officer advanced to the very edge of the pool and suddenly the six swimmers were joined by a spluttering Duty Officer trying to retrieve his hat and hang on to his sword without losing all his dignity. Nothing was ever proved as to who did what but the unfortunate Company Commander had a most uncomfortable interview soon after with a very angry Group Captain. All in a day's work!

HAVE A DRINK FROM THE BATTERY SILVER?

A Parachute Battalion Group was based in Bahrein throughout the early sixties as a fire brigade to reinforce the tiny Kuwait Army if Iraq tried to take over the country. This was 20 years before Sadam Hussein actually tried it. For political reasons the Group had to be based four hundred miles from the possible battle area since to appear actually on the spot would provide a 'provocation' and possibly precipitate an invasion.

The Bahreini offered a bare patch of sand ten miles from anywhere and the Battalion Group was left to get on with it. The principal element of the Group other than the Parachute Battalion was the Artillery Battery, which provided both the indirect fire support and the control of air strikes, there being a Hunter Fighter Ground Attack Squadron based at Muharraq Airfield which was connected to Bahrein proper by a causeway.

Unlike the Parachute Battalion, whose origins went back only as far as Winston Churchill's famous edict of 1940 'let there be a Para-chute Force of not less than 10,000 men . . .', the Battery could trace its history back to Waterloo and beyond; hence its full title of 'G' (Mercer's Troop) Parachute Battery, Royal Horse Artillery, of which every member of the unit was understandably proud.

The Regiments of long standing had all served in India in the 19th Century and had participated in such adventures as the rape of the Begums of Oudh, and the looting of the Princely Treasure Houses thereafter, hence their property books were stiff with elegant and priceless silver.

Recently raised Regiments had missed out on these colonial exploits and the Parachute Battalion was hard put to find more than a silver ash tray or two and perhaps a beer mug, in view of the price of modern silver. It was a great joy to the Gunners to quaff their pints from their splendid silver goblets, inscribed with their insignia and the Battle Honour Waterloo, while their colleagues in the Parachute Battalion were drinking beer straight from the can. It was considered the greatest honour for one of them to be invited to have a drink from the Battery silver (although it must be admitted that this did little to improve the taste of the dreadful Bahrein Beer).

As the tour of the Battalion Group neared its end and preparations were made to hand over the camp, looking quite ship-shape by now, to another outfit, the various Seconds in Command of the component units were sent back to the UK a few weeks early as an Advance Party.

The Battery Captain was charged with custody of the Battery Silver, which it had been decided to backload early. He lovingly packed each goblet in newspaper and laid them carefully in a cardboard 24-beer can box, of which there were many sculling around. He then went off to pay his farewell calls on the local 'brass' while his orderly finished his packing.

This young man was not overblessed with grey cells and coming upon the Battery Silver, concealed in newspaper within an old cardboard box, decided that this must be rubbish which his boss wished him to dispose of. Rather than take it to the dump at the far side of the camp, some two miles distant, he dumped it down the deep trench latrine used jointly by the Officers and Sergeants of the Group. By the time his boss returned and worked out what had happened to the precious silver, quite a number of Officers and Sergeants had made their daily contribution to the DTL.

The unfortunate orderly was lowered down by a series of toggle ropes but was unable to rescue the cardboard box with his feet. He was therefore summarily hauled up and put down again head first with firm instructions not to come up without the Battery Silver. This he eventually did and welcomed the services of two or three of his colleagues who were standing by to hose him down with buckets and stirrup pumps.

Long after this event when anyone from 1 PARA was asked if they would care to take a drink from the Battery Silver the answer was invariably the same, 'Thanks – but no thanks, I know where it's been!'

33

At Christmas 1963, the Greek and Turkish elements of what was then the unitary State of Cyprus, went for each other in an orgy of bloodletting. The two Battalions of British Troops resident in the Sovereign Base areas in the South of the Island were interposed, by agreement with both warring factions, as a 'Truce Force' along a 'Green Line' drawn with a blunt chinagraph pencil by the GOC, Major General Peter Young, which effectively divided the capital city of Nicosia along what was known as the Mason-Dixon line; Turks in the North and Greeks in the South.

Initially, the Truce Force was welcomed with open arms, as a similar force was to be welcomed in Londonderry in 1969, but relief at the cessation of open civil war quickly turned to suspicion and distrust as both sides realised that the Truce Force really was interposed to be impartial and not to further their own particular factional aims.

More and more British Battalions were brought in from the UK as the situation deteriorated to extend the Green Line and to monitor troublespots, of which there were many, in the hinterland. Among these was 1 PARA, which was deployed on the line from the City Centre eastwards to the fringe of the rural area, having been 'mobilised' on New Year's Eve without having previously been put on notice. All the soldiers made it except one who gave his leave address as the Playboy Hotel, Amsterdam.

One of the 'strategic' buildings garrisoned by 1 PARA was the Nicosia Cold Store, which had changed hands several times during the fighting over the Christmas period and which was tall enough to dominate the Green Line in both directions. Until the 'troubles' both Greek and Turkish merchants kept goods therein, but in the confusion of the fighting all the records had disappeared. It was rather like looking after the Quartermaster's Stores when someone had removed the ledgers, and 1 PARA took advantage of their opportunity in a modest way. Never had a Battalion been better fed. However, the Turkish enclave was virtually surrounded by Greek elements and around once a fortnight the Turks would mount an operation to effect a re-supply, probably from the goods of Turkish depositors lodged in the Cold Store.

It went something like this. Around midnight, the Turks would open fire over the Greek sector with their weapons carefully elevated to around 45 degrees. The Greeks would respond in the same manner and when the overhead fire was at its height, a small Turkish Task Force would enter the Cold Store with Bergens and wheelbarrows to stock up on provisions. Once they had enough for their immediate needs, the signal would be passed to the Turkish Commander who would then approach the British Representative to say that he would agree to a cease fire if the Greeks would. This intelligence was passed to the Truce Force Representative with the Greeks, who, after a few more bursts of tracer, just to make their point, agreed also. The war was over (for a time) and the Truce Force chalked up another success in peacekeeping before everyone went back to bed!

This worked well enough when the Truce Force was under British Command and Rules of Engagement. On those occasions when British positions were being consistently sniped from either side, a few well-placed rounds in return, through the next window, rather than that used by the Sniper, usually did the trick. On one occasion a 120mm MOBAT anti-tank gun was lined up at a particularly troublesome nest of snipers. The thought of a HESH round landing in their midst brought an immediate cooling of their ardour.

Sadly, this state of affairs did not survive the translation of the Truce Force into UN Troops. As British, it was possible to require either or both sides to stay on their own side of a line or to desist from a given action, e.g. sniping, and to back this up – or at least threaten to do so – with appropriate force. Once the Blue Beret was donned, one could only make a request to the local commander with the ultimate sanction of a report of non-compliance to the UN in New York, 5,000 miles away. This meant less than nothing to the local leader on the ground and the situation rapidly worsened.

British Troops, numbering some seven Battalions, were progressively relieved by contingents from nations which had agreed to place forces under UN Command, until ultimately only one British Unit, plus an Armoured Recce Squadron and Logistic Support Troops, remained. During this rundown, 1 PARA, having handed over their Sector to the Van Doos (R 22e R), who were old hands at UN peacekeeping, were moved to Force Reserve. Not unnaturally, after six months active operations, the off-duty Companies sought out the Charwallah's compound and had a ball. Later, after the Standby Company had been deployed to some crisis near Timbou and the next Company in line had deployed to another near Peristerona, D Company Commander worked out that it was his turn next and sent out fast running coolies to all corners of the camp with a warning order.

Sadly, they had little effect, particularly since the Sergeant Major and all his Senior NCOs had booked out to investigate a cat house in the South of the City which the Company had searched for weapons on a previous operation. Sure enough, within a few minutes, D Coy was re-called to duty and what could be found of the O Group stumbled off to the Battalion Ops Room for a briefing. 'The Irish have arrived,' said the Ops Officer by way of introduction, 'You mean the IRA?' asked someone. 'No, no. The Army of the Irish Republic,' he replied testily, 'and they're tired – go and unload their aircraft.'

This was greeted with incredulity initially, since when the British Army arrive anywhere, some unfortunate Lance Corporal and six soldiers are pressed into duty to unload the aircraft; never mind about being tired. After a few more acrimonious exchanges with the Ops Officer, D Company, less its Senior NCOs, who were still engaged in other activities, mounted their vehicles and left for the airport, practically all suffering from a surfeit of alcohol.

On arrival, they were met by the spectacle of the Irish Contingent, with their funny zig-zag rank stripes, lined up on Parade and Presenting Arms to the UN Force Commander who had come to welcome them, one General Gyani by name, a most distinguished Officer of the Indian Army and known to the troops, perhaps inevitably, as the Chief Charwallah.

What the Company Commander had not appreciated was that the Sergeant of 10 Platoon, a confirmed Ulsterman, had something on the Battalion Chief Clerk (over drink or women, maybe both) and had induced him to accumulate every Northern Irishman in the Battalion in his Platoon. The effect of this was immediately apparent when the Company debussed on the fringe of the Irish Contingent's arrival ceremony. 10 Platoon, having drink taken, opened up a barrage of barracking indicating in no uncertain fashion that they regarded their compatriots from the South as 'F – – rebels' and giving a stirring rendering of 'The Sash', whose significance was lost on those not familiar with the Ulster scene. In the face of this quite dramatic intervention, the Irish were not quite sure whether to continue to Present Arms or load live and take on this unexpected intrusion by what was clearly a nest of Orangemen.

General Gyani looked mystified, as well he might, and the Company Commander, having spent the past six months negotiating to keep the peace between Greek and Turk, suddenly found the technique vital by quickly interposing between Northern and Southern Irish.

Eventually calm was restored, the welcome ceremony was completed and the Irish departed for work-up training at Dhekelia. Soon afterwards the Company Commander, helping to supervise the unloading of the USAF Globemasters, was approached by a runner from 10 Platoon who asked, in the unmistakeable accent of the Shanklin Road, if the Officers would prefer Irish or Scotch Whisky. This sort of question required a degree of investigation and, on being pressed, the soldier replied that 10 Platoon had just unloaded the 'sorplies' for the Irish Officers' Mess and were in the process of redistribution. There are times when a Company Commander should not dig too deeply into how his Company achieves its tasks – and this was one of them. Complaints followed, of course, but the already enormous bureaucracy of the UN Headquarters absorbed most before they ever reached the Battalion.

The sequel was the arrival of the Swedish Contingent a few days later when, bored with being in reserve, D Company actually volunteered for aircraft unloading duties. They came on parade with all the tools acquired during six months active operations in an urban area, bolt cutters, hacksaws, monkey wrenches – even an oxyacetylene torch acquired from somewhere by the ever-versatile Sergeant of 10 Platoon. Sadly, the Company were disappointed. The Swedes arrived dry. They may drink like fishes once they deploy to their opcon area but they don't bring booze with them. The only items which D Company admired were the rather smart Air Force (or UN) blue coloured shirts which buttoned down at the collar points, which the Swedes, old hands at UN operations, all wore. The next morning D Company appeared on Muster Parade with every single man wearing a smart blue shirt with a button down collar. 'Sergeant Major,' said the Company Commander, 'where's my bloody shirt?' 'Ah, Sir,' he replied, 'there's a selection for you and the other Officers in my office.' The Company Commander, appreciating the situation, decided that the traditional solutions are often the best in time of doubt, and gave the time-honoured response which has served Company Commanders so well through the ages, 'Carry on Sar-nt-Major.'

The frustrations of UN operations can be many but the ingenuity, good humour and initiative of the British Soldier never fails to carry him through whatever is thrown at him. It was a privilege to serve with him.

"OK, chaps. Fall out for a smoke."

6

Peacetime Soldiering

KNOW YOUR LIMITATIONS

In the sixties, Aldershot District was commanded by a fiery General who thirsted for more challenging activity than peacetime administration provided. He decided to carry out the Annual Inspections of all his Battalions in person rather than delegating these to his staff, as was usual.

Before he started his round of inspections, he assembled all the officers and gave them due warning of what to expect, the nub of his exhortation being that they should know their men. 'When I was a young Officer,' he said, 'I got seven days extra Orderly Officer for not knowing how many left-handed Methodists I had in my Platoon.' The assembled multitudes took due note. Some went round their men asking if they were left-handed Methodists. The more intelligent realised that they had to learn every detail about them and some spent hours memorising where they came from and what their special interests were, as well as their purely military skills.

One particular Platoon Commander had the greatest difficulty in all this. His memory was not of the best and it was all he could do to learn the name of his men, let alone everything else. His Platoon Sergeant solved the problem as Sergeants have done throughout the ages. 'Whatever the Officer says,' he told the Platoon, 'you back him up whether it's right or wrong.' The Platoon nodded. They were used to the strange ways in which the Army conducted its affairs.

Eventually the day came when the General inspected 1 PARA. He went through the Battalion like a dose of salts, finally arriving at the Young Officer's Platoon. After a few preliminary questions, all of which he answered successfully, he stopped before one particular soldier. 'What's his name?' asked the General. 'Morris, Sir,' replied the Platoon Commander (correctly). 'And where does he come from?' persisted the General. 'Er – Er Worthing, Sir,' said the young Officer, clutching a place name out of thin air. 'Well Morris,' said the General turning to the soldier. 'Do you come from Worthing?' Morris was quick on the uptake as befits a parachute soldier. 'Shurre an' Begorra, Surr. Oi've lived in Worthing all me loife.'

"If your ancestors were at Hastings I can see why we lost!"

IT PAYS TO WORK THE SYSTEM

During the sixties, the annual Combined Cadet Force Rifle Meeting at Bisley was run as a separate event and not, as it is now, buttoned on to the main Army Meeting. The performance took a Rifle Company to run it, which was virtually written off for a week, putting up the tents, taking over and distributing bedding, manning the catering facilities and, most onerous of all, manning the butts and most of the firing points on the famous Century Range.

In the year that D Company 1 PARA drew the short straw for

this commitment, some nine hundred cadets were expected to attend. On the day before they assembled for their shooting competition, a ten tonner appeared from the local Ordnance Depot bearing, amongst other things, nine hundred pure pristine mattresses, brand new and straight from the manufacturers.

The eyes of the Company Colour Sergeant lit up at the sight. Every Battalion in the area had a number of 'soiled mattresses' usually referred to as 'p----d' although sometimes they were simply marked by boot polish or rifle oil. In any event, once a mattress was classed as soiled it couldn't be exchanged and someone, usually the unit if the individual couldn't be identified, had to pay over £50, which mounts up if one is dealing in a multiple of mattresses.

The Colour Sergeant made a few calls to selected chums and within minutes Army trucks appeared from all points of the compass bearing 'p----d' mattresses from every unit in the Aldershot area, which were promptly exchanged for new ones.

After the Rifle Meeting, the Company Commander summoned the local Ordnance Officer to examine the mattresses before they were returned to the Depot. 'Can't understand it,' he said, after inspecting the evidence. 'Out of nine hundred and seven cadets, nine hundred and six have p----d their mattresses! Well, they're not subject to Military Law so we can't charge them a penny. Burn the bloody lot!'

Thus it was that the credit of the Colour Sergeant of a certain Parachute Rifle Company was good for months thereafter and many were the favours called in as a quid pro quo for this imaginative administrative sleight of hand.

IMAGINATIVE EXERCISES CAN BECOME TOO REALISTIC

During the mid sixties, between mini-crises in Cyprus and Aden, 1 PARA were used frequently on a 'rent-an-enemy' basis by units in what was then called Southern Command.

From a company-level viewpoint, these activities seemed to resolve round Salisbury Plain. D Company was wont to drop on Everleigh DZ, usually at last light hoping the RAF navigators had got their sums right, since if they were a bit over-eager and dropped early, the first jumpers to leave the aircraft landed in the pig farm adjoining the dropping zone – and stank to high heaven for days. Having dropped, they would either attack Sidbury Hill, the most prominent feature at the west end of the Plain, or defend it – according to the scenario. It became so much of a routine that the Sergeant Major would ask the Company Commander, 'Shall we use the same trenches we occupied on the last three exercises – or dig some new ones?'

The prospect of a major NATO exercise called LINK WEST (for no obvious reason) which was to range over the whole of the UK, was greeted with a degree of enthusiasm; at least it might be something different! The opening narrative was hardly typical 'The World is at War and D Company is in the Gas Works'.

The exercise involved a simulated attack on the UK. 1 PARA deployed to Warcop and then to Catterick, both well known military training areas, dealing with incidents involving minor enemy infiltration by what, in later years, came to be called SPETZNAZ forces plus a degree of simulated subversion by enemy sympathisers at key points.

"Fire two more fer effect. I'm makin' a stovepipe."

42

The climax of the phase based on Catterick was a company operation on the guard room of a Signal Training Regiment in Catterick Camp, where 'good guys' had been incarcerated by 'bad guys'. All very straight-forward stuff. Capture the area, release our friends and lock up our enemies.

D Company went in just before first light, which was around 0400 hrs, and overcame the token resistance with surprising ease, duly releasing the prisoners – who appeared to be thoroughly mystified by the whole affair – and locking up their guards.

What was not apparent, until later, was that there were no less than three Signal Regiments in Catterick Camp and D Company had 'sprung' the wrong one, releasing genuine soldiers under sentence and locking up the real regimental police. (It took some days to re-capture all the released prisoners who made the best of their unexpected freedom.)

The unfortunate Company Commander was cast as the sacrificial lamb and spent many hours apologising to the CO of the Signal Regiment, the Signal Brigade Commander, the Garrison Commander and Uncle Tom Cobley and all. You clearly can't win 'em all.

TO BE A GENERAL'S DAUGHTER

The mid sixties found 16 Parachute Brigade occupying so-called modern barracks in Aldershot. Each Officer's mess was an identical three-tier matchbox and 1 PARA lived in the last one of a complex of four, the others being occupied by Brigade HQ, 2 PARA and 3 PARA. By some quirk of the plumbing, all the Messes were connected laterally so that all the hot water was drained off by the other users long before it reached 1 PARA.

The unwashed subalterns were muttering and the situation was becoming impossible; hence the PMC called a Council of War to seek a solution. It so happened that the Adjutant was a handsome and debonair Officer, much sought after by the local ladies (he had a slight limp, following an injury to both ankles, having had to bail out from a Nursing Officer's bedroom on the second floor of the RAF Hospital Aden when the Matron entered unexpectedly).

The Council of War decided to capitalise on the Adjutant's charm to solve their hot water problem. He was invited to make approaches to Sara, the General's daughter; an attractive but formidable young lady whose suitors were normally put off by the seniority and remoteness of her distinguished parent. However, the Adjutant was an Officer of considerable determination, as well as his many other attributes, and he pursued Sara relentlessly. Eventually, as anticipated, he was invited to drinks at Government House by the General. After some small talk he was asked the inevitable 'Senior Officer taking an interest-type question'. 'How are things in 1 PARA my boy?' 'Ah Sir,' said the Adjutant, 'there is a slight problem,' and went on to explain about the hot water.

Within 2 hours the PSA were crawling all over the 1 PARA Mess and the hot water was instantly restored by reversing a misplaced valve.

1 PARA were happy – and Sara was immediately dropped. There are distinct disadvantages to being a General's daughter!

ALWAYS HANDLE CLERICAL STAFF WITH CARE

44 Parachute Brigade was entirely a TA organisation with a tiny staff of regular army officers and NCOs to support its training and administration. The logistic element consisted of two regular officers, a Staff Sergeant Chief Clerk and a civilian clerk/typist who was of Afro-Caribbean descent and rejoiced in the nick-name of Lumumba since his own was completely unpronounceable.

It was not unusual for all the officers to be away from Brigade Headquarters in London either planning a training exercise or visiting one of the units spread nationwide throughout the UK. It was on one such occasion that Lumumba chose to throw a wobbler and refused to carry on typing. The Chief Clerk was a man of few words, 'Carry on or I'll thump you,' Lumumba didn't – so he did.

Realising that he had better obtain some protective cover in case the union became involved, the Chief Clerk rang the TAVRA Secretary, a retired Brigadier of enormous experience, and explained his problem. The Secretary was equally loath to let a problem moulder on. He interviewed both in turn and finally

44

called them into his office together. 'It's all been an unfortunate misunderstanding,' he advised. 'I want you both to shake hands then go and have a drink together.' The Chief Clerk was quite happy with this and so apparently was Lumumba. 'Sah,' he said, 'I go 'long with dat, no problem. But Ah have no money. Please lend me five pounds.'

What the Secretary said was not reported but it became irrelevant since Lumumba was charged by the civil police soon afterwards with selling driving licences, at a price, to his countrymen. It transpired that he had managed to lift a book of blank 'pass' forms from his previous TA unit when it was disbanded and was doing a roaring trade in illicit sales. He was rumbled, as is often the case, by a clerical error, when he filled in the wrong group and authorised the proud possessor to drive a 'track-laying vehicle steered by the tracks'. If you're on the fiddle, it pays to be careful.

NOT ALL MARCH HARES ARE MAD!

In the mid sixties, 44 Parachute Brigade set up an annual escape and evasion exercise for parachute units and selected visitors from the Royal Navy and Royal Air Force.

The concept was to drop the evaders by night in ones and twos on a North-South road across a remote part of the Yorkshire Moors, from whence they had to reach points on the coast, some 40 miles away, where they would notionaly be picked up by a friendly submarine 48 hours later.

The Hunter Force, representing the occupying power out to capture the evaders, was formed from three Regiments from the Royal Signals Training Brigade at Catterick, supplemented by a Detachment of the US Special Forces (Green Berets) from Bad Tolz in Bavaria.

Those who were captured were handed over to the Interrogation Training Wing from the Intelligence Corps Depot, which had the task of training those who would, in a real war situation, be charged with the tactical questioning of prisoners. These were tough customers, many with war-time experience, who gave the captured evaders a hard time to induce them to give

45

information on their unit and its role. One particular ploy was to blindfold a bunch of prisoners, take them for a flight in an aircraft and then put them in a wing of the detention centre where the guards wore soviet uniforms, the notices in the cells were in Russian and even the cutlery bore red army identification numbers.

Even after as little as twenty-four hours, deprived of sleep and with little or no food, most prisoners became disoriented and prone to let slip some fragment of information. This was seized upon and followed up during other interrogations and it was amazing how much of an intelligence picture could be built up over a relatively short time by skilled interrogators.

The principal duty of the Deputy Chief of Staff, who in those days was called the Deputy Assistant Adjutant and Quartermaster General, terminology which had not changed since the days of Wellington, was to keep track of the invaders as individuals so that at the end of the exercise the Brigade Commander could be sure that they were all accounted for and that none had been left, dying of exposure or whatever, on the moors.

On one occasion, mirabile dictu, he ended up with two more than he started with. This was theoretically impossible and an immediate investigation was started. Fortunately, someone remembered that one of the groups of prisoners given the Russian treatment had contained two evaders who not only had not given any information but even failed to understand the questions. They were either very clever or very stupid and were at that moment undergoing their final interrogation. It transpired that there is a nature trail across the Yorkshire Moors called the Lyke Wake Walk and the two additional evaders were not soldiers at all but members of a Rambling Club who happened to have started their trek during the hours of darkness and had been captured. After almost two days of being in the hands of what they firmly believed to be the KGB, they were only too ready to sign a disclaimer to virtually anything. They were reasonable men and after a good meal and a talk with the Brigadier, they took it all in good part and the matter never became an issue; at least it never hit the Press. Good thing they weren't CND sympathisers.

The next problem on this particular exercise was what to do with the A Team from the US Special Forces. Their aircraft was not due to pick them up until 36 hours later and they clearly had to be given hospitality. Eventually it was agreed to send them to London by train to stay at 44 Parachute Brigade Headquarters at the Duke of York HQ in Chelsea. Two Londoner Senior NCOs were detailed to accompany them to 'show them the town'.

This must have worked reasonably well since the next to be heard of their activities was when the Secretary of Greater London TAVRA, an Officer of enormous distinction, called on the Parachute Brigadier to complain. He had insomnia, he explained, and while walking his dog round the Duke of York's running track at about 4am, he was surprised to see a completely naked lady emerge from the 44 Parachute Brigade Headquarters pursued by an equally naked American soldier, or so he presumed from the interchange of dialogue when he caught her, to be carried back into the building for undisclosed purposes. The TAVRA Secretary was not one to protest too much, he said, but perhaps the US visitors could be rather more circumspect in the future.

The next year following the same exercise, the Deputy Chief of Staff lodged the US visitors with the Parachute Engineer Squadron in Kingsbury – and not a peep was heard. Presumably in that part of North London it is less unusual for naked people to pursue each other in the early hours of the morning!

TELL ME CONFIDENTIALLY, ARE YOUR FEET COLD?

44 Parachute Brigade (TA) always had a full establishment of Chaplains, men in Holy Orders who enjoyed the challenge of Airborne Operations and the close contact with volunteer soldiers from every strata of society.

Every year they had a 'Retreat' at which they considered things temporal and spiritual for a few days mid week, so that they could be back to their flock or their TA unit (or both) at the weekend.

One particularly enterprising Senior Padre decided to hold this Annual Retreat in Snowdonia where his Padres could indulge in a little muscular christianity, climbing mountains, to complement their theological studies.

The Chief Administrative Officer of 44 Parachute Brigade went to assist this group (what is the collective noun for an assembly of chaplains? – a pride of parsons perhaps!) to see how they were progressing and, more importantly perhaps, to settle their bill at the Pen-y-Gwrhyd pub where they were staying.

After a day on the mountain with them, this officer (whose title was then Deputy Assistant Adjutant and Quartermaster General – which, after all, was good enough in Wellington's day – now it's abbreviated to DCOS G1/G4, which has nothing like the same ring to it) was invited to join them at their final Dinner, which had traditionally become known as the Last Supper. This was something of an eye opener. The Padres had appointed one of their number as the Treasurer – or Keeper of the Pieces of Silver, as they called him – who had worked out their allowances to the last penny. 'We can have trifle and coffee or skip the sweet and have a large brandy instead. Choose!' Guess what they selected.

It was a Friday night and it so happened that the DAA and QMG had to be back in Aldershot on the Saturday morning to join a Brigade Exercise, so he decided to drive south through the night, joined by one of the Padres with a London parish who had a full programme of weddings and funerals on the morrow. They took it in turns to drive the rather clapped-out Landrover and were just leaving the Coventry area on the M45 when they were flagged down by the local police. The DQ rolled out of the passenger seat to ask what was the problem. 'Speeding,' said the police; 'Did you know you were doing 40 in a built-up area?' 'You'd better ask the

Padre,' replied the DQ, 'he's driving!' 'Padre?' said the police, 'a likely story.' At this point the Padre entered the lists with his hands clasped in the praying position.

Having blessed everyone within sight, he then started on a yarn so far fetched that even the DQ, who had heard a tale or two in his time, was impressed. The upshot was that instead of being charged, the police couldn't have been more helpful. 'Of course we understand, Padre,' they said. 'You must be in Bermondsey for a christening at first light. Allow us to escort you to the end of our territory,' and the little group went led by the police car with blue light flashing.

Moral – if you want to exceed the speed limit with immunity, take a Padre along.

"HIT ANY KEY TO CONTINUE"

7

Retreat from Empire

During the confrontation between Indonesia and Malaysia in the mid-sixties, the SAS Squadrons who kept watch on the Borneo border became over-stetched and each Parachute Battalion formed a 'Patrol' Company to supplement their efforts.

Each four-man patrol operated from a firm base well back from the border ridge which was manned by an element of one of the British or Malaysian Infantry Battalions.

The Company Commander of D Coy 1 PARA was making a whistle-stop tour of all the patrol bases in his operational area on taking over from his predecessor. On arrival at one patrol base manned by a Platoon of what was then the Royal Uster Rifles, the Company Commander's helicopter descended on to the landing strip to be met by the Pengulu (Headman) of the local tribe, who had clearly been mobilised to meet the visiting VIP.

This gentleman, clad only in a loin cloth, stepped forward, banged the butt of his spear on the ground and greeted the Company Commander in very passable English. 'Good morning Sir – and F...k the Pope.' Clearly his idea of a formal introduction.

The Irish never lose the chance of making their point.

COMPUTERS CAN BE USER FRIENDLY

1 PARA was among the last Infantry Battalions to leave Aden, having served through the several months prior to the final withdrawal when the anti-British terrorist campaign was at its height.

Battalions at that time divided naturally into 'gentlemen', who kept a low profile and hoped to lead a quiet life, and 'players', who sought to dominate their operational area and to confront the terrorists head on. 1 PARA was a 'player' Battalion.

Several successful operations in Sheik Othman and Dar Said netted 1 PARA several clutches of prisoners whose interrogation produced more information which, in turn, led to more successful actions on the snowball principle.

Sadly, there were those in high places who did not entirely approve of 'player' Battalions and in particular of the vigorous interrogation methods employed by 1 PARA. It was made quite clear that if any more prisoners were shot 'trying to escape' or damaged by 'accidentally falling downstairs' a full investigation would be initiated, from which, it was hinted, dire consequences would follow.

Clearly, it was time for a rethink. The continued flow of information was vital to enable 1 PARA to retain the initiative and reduce the loss of British lives to the minimum but how to achieve this without bringing down the wrath of the establishment was the problem. The Second-in-Command, Adjutant and Intelligence Officer, got their heads together and came up with an idea.

Just prior to the situation becoming virtually impossible in terms of normal commerce, the Chartered Bank had taken delivery of a main-frame computer, an enormous piece of electronic wizardry which represented the state of the art at that time. A request punched in would give rise to much whirring of wheels, grinding of gears and flashing of multi-coloured lights. After some twenty minutes or so this monster would bring forth a mouse in the form of a bank statement or some similar minor document.

Happily, 1 PARA had an OP on the roof of the Bank since its height dominated the surrounding area and thus classified it as a 'strategic building'. 1 PARA had access to the roof and, perhaps less directly, to the computer.

A simple method of interrogation was evolved under which a terrorist was lashed to the main-frame and informed that the radiation from the machine would make him sterile, Arabs being particularly sensitive about their macho image. A programme was then run with all the whirrings and grindings and flashing of lights concomitant with producing a slip of paper some minutes later. This was then torn up in front of the terrorist and he was informed that the right one was now drained. Would he care to talk or should the left suffer the same fate. Some did at this point but for those who chose not to, the procedure was repeated.

After the second bank statement had been torn up, a large alarm clock was produced and the terrorist informed that the process was reversible but he only had ten minutes before it became final. Would he care to talk? He had now nine minutes . . . eight . . . seven . . . Had he got children? Too bad. He'd never any now . . . six . . . five . . . four . . .

It didn't work for ever but a remarkable amount of information was gleaned and from it 1 PARA were able to foil two ambushes, uncover several ammo dumps and round up a most satisfactory number of terrorists' contacts and cut outs.

The domination of 1 PARA's operational area was continued and the interrogated terrorists were handed over to the RAF Police, who ran the detention centre, in pristine condition albeit a touch pale and shaken. The soldiers of 1 PARA, who benefited from the information gained, all developed a warm feeling for that computer. It really was 'user friendly'.

The first phase of the British withdrawal from Aden in 1967, was the evacuation of Little Aden, custom built as a British Brigade Base and only completed a few months previously, no doubt at vast expense. The Headquarters of 24 Infantry Brigade and most of its units returned directly from Little Aden to the UK but the 1st Battalion IRISH GUARDS were transferred to the Aden Brigade to act as a Force Reserve (or, as they put it themselves, as hostages to fortune).

Companies of the new Battalion were farmed out to the existing units of the Aden Brigade as reinforcements and to gain experience of operating in an urban enviroment. One of these came to 1 PARA. The PARA 'Toms' viewed the Guards with some disdain. They thought the men were probably all right although sadly lacking in initiative by PARA standards, but they had a poor opinion of their officers, whom they felt were epitomised by the caricature of the mythical guards officer 'ffearfully-ffearfully-Chinless' with four small fs and two hyphens.

In the early hours of one sultry morning when all of Shaik Othman, terrorists included, seemed to be fast asleep, the radio net heard one OP, manned by the Irish Guards and clearly bored stiff, whispering to another. 'Hello Oscar Four, this is Oscar One. Do ye come from Dublin? Over.' The reply came, 'Hello Oscar One, this is Oscar Four. Shure oi come from Dublin. Woi? Over.' 'Hello Oscar Four. This is Oscar one. Well, I come from f...... Belfast. Out.' And the night was rent by a long burst of machine gun fire from one OP to the other.

The Irish always find it difficult to discard their domestic disputes.

OPERATION BIG LIFT

During the first five months of their tour in the Middle East in mid 1967, 1 PARA was responsible for Sheikh Othmann, a suburb of Aden.

The operational development involved the permanent occupa-

53

pation of a number of OPs on a series of dominating buildings. These provided both observation into most of the potential trouble spots and also firm bases to support patrols moving through the streets.

The most vulnerable and exposed OP was that located in the tower of the Sheikh Othman Police Station. It was surrounded on three sides by high buildings all of which could be, and frequently were, used as firing points to engage the Police Station and other OPs in the area. Since the Police Station was in the geographical centre of the township its occupation by Security Forces was a constant reminder to the terrorists that 'Big Brother', in the form of 1 PARA, was watching them and their attacks on it became more and more vicious. The Civil Police were powerless in the face of heavily armed terrorists and were convinced that they would be unable to prevent the terrorists from burning the Police Station if its garrison was withdrawn. It thus became a point of high politics that the Police Station must be held at all costs as its sacking by terrorists would give an inestimable boost to their morale and demonstrate to the world at large that the British could no longer contain the situation in Aden.

The normal garrison of what was known as OP4 was a half platoon of 12-14 men under an officer. The tower itself was always manned by four men, although this was increased in times of crisis, and the reliefs slept on the first floor of the main building. The Civil Police, with whom relations remained cordial, confined their activities to the ground floor which was surrounded by a high wall and was not therefore vulnerable to direct small arms attack.

The usual defensive measures were taken to make the position as strong as possible and 60 Fd Sqn RE built the equivalent of a fort on the top of the tower, with two loop holes facing each point of the compass.

While the defence of OP4 against small arms was as good as could be devised, the garrison began to suffer casualties from blindicide rockets, a Czech wapon of the bazooka family, of which the terrorists seemed to have plenty. There were several direct hits on the tower culminating in one particularly unlucky shot which hit a corner post and all four of the duty watch became casualties. Happily, only one was serious and they all subsequently recovered.

A device which had proved successful elsewhere was a 'blindicide screen' of rigid wire mesh which exploded the rockets on impact so that the force of the explosion was dissipated and only the splinters hit the defences proper. The difficulty at OP4 was to fit such a screen over the fighting floor of the tower. This was difficult enough from the purely engineering aspect but to attempt to carry out the construction work involved, much of it exposed to fire, would have invited an unacceptable number of casualties.

The obvious solution was to construct the screen on a frame as a complete unit and lower the whole thing over the tower by helicopter. A representative of 13 Flight, Army Air Corps had a look at the problem and decided that it was a starter provided the all up weight was such that it could be lifted by a Scout, i.e. less than 1000 lbs.

Working to these limits, 60 Fd Sqn quickly produced a birdcage-like structure out of tubular scaffolding and wire mesh. Then the whole thing was lifted by a Scout of 13 Flight on to a mock-up tower in a safe area by way of a rehearsal. In spite of misgivings by the pilot as to how the 'thing' would fly, the trial was a success and the operation to install it was arranged for the following morning.

The time selected was first light as this was a time normally free of terrorist incidents, the theory being that they liked to lie in after their strenuous activities against British positions on the previous evening. It was hoped that, by taking off in the darkness and appearing over Sheikh Otham as the dawn was breaking, the operation would be over before the duty terrorist had time to rouse his comrades and get them into action.

Nevertheless, on the principle that helicopters, like armour, must have infantry protection when likely to make contact with the enemy at close range, two companies of 1 PARA were deployed one hour before first light on to the roof tops of Sheikh Othman along the route to be flown by the Scout. A command element comprising a senior pilot and the Battalion 2IC positioned themselves on the roof of an abandoned police married quarter and a team of sappers took up their positions in the tower itself, ready to guide the 'thing' into position.

Promptly at first light the Scout appeared, flew over the surprised inhabitants of Sheikh Othman, and hovered over the

Police Station. The sapper team quickly caught the trailing guide ropes and after only one false start the Scout got the 'thing' in the right position. The pilot on the ground passed the word to drop to the Scout and the 'thing' came to rest within a few inches of its designated position – a very skilful piece of flying indeed. Surprise was complete and the Scout and covering troops withdrew without incident while the sappers carried out a few fine adjustments.

The 'thing' proved most successful and although many more blindicides were fired at OP4 no further casualties were suffered. It was still going strong when 1 PARA handed over the Sheikh Othman area to the South Arabian Army.

Operation Big Lift was an excellent example of what can be achieved by inventive minds, skilful flying, good timing and plain old fashioned guts. The companies of 1 PARA, all of whom manned OP4 on rotation, were most grateful to 60 Fd Sqn RE and 13 Flt AAC whose high standards of professional skill enabled the operation to be mounted and conducted successfully.

VIP VISITORS CAN BE A *PAIN*!

During the final phase of the withdrawal from Aden, the remaining British Battalions formed a tight perimeter round the city and its airfield. Most of the VIPs from the Middle East Command Headquarters had gone home since their sphere of influence, which had once embraced virtually the whole of South Arabia, was reduced to a few map squares. Nonetheless, there were a few who elected to remain with the 'chee-aps' till the bitter end but, having virtually nothing to do, took to visiting the final defensive positions on a regular basis.

One particular VIP, who was a keen horseman, had liberated three arab stallions from the former Aden Jockey Club stables and took to descending on the British line on horseback escorted by two troopers, requisitioned from the Armoured Recce Squadron of the Queens Own Hussars who provided the Force Mobile Reserve.

One of the positions occupied by 1 PARA had an extensive field of fire over flat desert terrain and this became a favourite stopping point for the VIP and his entourage. It reminded him of Tobruk, he said, where, as a young gunner officer, he had placed a red barrel at 1,000 metres, a blue one at 1,500 metres and a green one at 2,000 metres and so on. When the Germans attacked he could estimate their exact range by referring to the barrels and bring down heavy 'fire for effect'.

1 PARA were quick to appreciate the parallel and the next time the VIP came riding by there was a red barrel at 1,000 metres, a blue at 1,500 and a green at 2,000. This encouraged the VIP enormously and enhanced the reputation of 1 PARA in what was left of Command Headquarters.

What was not appreciated was that barrels were a highly negotiable asset in Aden and, came the dawn, the locals had pinched the lot. Thereafter, the sole task of the Sergeant Major of Support Company, whose detachments had all been farmed out to the Rifle Companies, together with his Company Clerk and Storeman, was to monitor the Command net and listen for a particular code word which heralded the imminent approach of the VIP. He would then drive off into the desert with a truck full of coloured barrels, lobbing one off at 1,000 metres, another at 1,500 and so on, going to ground in a deep dune until the VIP suitably impressed by the imitation of his Tobruk experiences, had moved on. The Sergeant Major and his team then reversed the process and picked up the barrels before the locals could spirit them away.

It may not, as the French Commander in the Crimea was wont to say, have been war – but it kept 1 PARA amused and kept the VIP off their backs.

RADIO SECURITY IS IMPORTANT

During the final phase of the withdrawal from Aden, the British Battalions came under attack from Energa grenades fired by the various terrorist factions. These were a British made anti-tank grenade fired from a launcher fixed to a rifle muzzle and propelled by an uprated blank known as a balastite cartridge. The whole of the Middle East reserve stock of Energa grenades had been taken over by the Egyptians following the Suez débâcle and issued, or perhaps sold, to any anti British organisation that wished to acquire them.

One particular faction in Aden had obviously not paid attention when being taught lesson one on the Energa since they invariably prepared the grenade for firing with the detonator, which had an open end and a closed end, the wrong way round. This rendered the grenades harmless and they bounced off armoured vehicles or defensive positions with no harm done.

All went well until one of the stations of a newly-arrived Battalion, apparently not realising that the command radio net could be intercepted by any terrorist with a taxi radio or other shortwave receiver, came on the air to report, 'We have just been under attack by Energa grenades. No damage or casualties. As usual, the detonators were put in the wrong way round!' Bingo! The very same night several positions were attacked by Energa grenades with the detonators assembled correctly and casualties sustained.

The offending Battalion won the Aden Brigade unpopularity contest outright as a result.

HAS ANYONE SEEN MY SHIP?

In the last few weeks before the British finally withdrew from Aden, there was a period of relative peace. The handover of the main base at Little Aden and the obvious preparations for total withdrawal finally convinced the two main terrorist groups that the British really were leaving and, as a result, they concentrated their activities on each other rather than on the remaining British.

The final defensive line, styled the 'Pennine Chain' in the way the Army has of giving everything a code-name, enclosed little more than the town itself and the Khormaksah Airfield; an area relatively easy to defend as most of the perimeter stretched across the salt pans and marshes with excellent fields of fire.

1 PARA held the key north eastern sector of this position, which included the two main axes along which any attack on the Pennine Chain would have to be routed. While their positions were well dug in and wired, the nature of the terrain made them almost invisible from the air and 1 PARA were concerned that the fighter ground attack pilots from HMS Eagle, which had appeared

from the Far East to provide air cover for the final withdrawal, would launch their attack, should this prove necessary, on an advancing enemy and not on the positions occupied by 1 PARA. A ground recce was clearly essential to give the fly-boys a good look around, which would, hopefully, enable them to direct any air attacks on to the correct target, or at least not on to 1 PARA.

In the funny way these things happen, the Second-in-Command had been at Sandhurst with Eagle's Ground Liaison Officer and a quick ship-to-shore radio conversation arranged for the attack pilots to be flown ashore by helicopter to spend a day going round the Pennine Chain. It so happened that the Aden Guardship and maid of all work, a Minesweeper of the Ton Class, was commanded by an experienced Naval Aviator Lieutenant Commander, who was getting his ticket punched as a ship driver; essential for his promotion to Commander. He had previously flown from Eagle and had also strong links with 1 PARA, formed during an earlier tour as Naval Support Liaison Officer on a series of exercises in the Gulf. He heard the radio arrangements being made for the pilots' visit to 1 PARA and chimed in to ask that the helicopter pick him up too from the RFA Ammunition ship anchored next to his own. Before leaving, he told his First Lieutenant that he hadn't bothered to clear his unforeseen 'shore leave' with the Admiral and that he expected him to react, as a good subordinate should, to any signals from the Flag.

The visit duly went ahead and 1 PARA took all the pilots round their positions, mostly on foot but with a foray into the nearest bazaar so that they could equip themselves with mini NLF flags, then the current 'I was there!' souvenir. Overall the visit was a great success and the reserve company was detailed to entertain the pilots for a late lunch. Happily, they had brought a case of duty free gin from Eagle and the late lunch became more and more prolonged. The helicopter returning for them at 3 o'clock was waved away and told to return at 4. The same thing happened at 4 and it was not until 5 o'clock that a bunch of well-oiled fighter pilots and one minesweeper Captain were assisted into their helicopter for the return to the Eagle.

Having dropped the pilots at Eagle, the Captain asked the helicopter to return him to his ship, but Lo – no Minesweeper; just an empty patch of sea.

On landing on the RFA and enquiring what had happened, the unfortunate Commanding Officer was told, 'Oh, haven't you heard? The Admiral sent her to Mombasa!'

There can't be many occasions when a helicopter has flown off into the sunset bearing an anxious Captain leaning from the door metaphorically singing out 'Has anybody seen my ship?'

How it all turned out was not known to 1 PARA but the gallant Captain was promoted Commander on the next List and survived to wear his brasshat – which can't be bad!

IF YOU'VE GOT IT, FLAUNT IT!

During the final phase of the withdrawal from Aden, the Military Secretary (MS), a distinguished General on the point of retiring, left his London desk to have a last look at Aden, where he had served as a young Officer and, to justify his trip, to brief the several Star Officers at what was then still termed Middle East Command Headquarters on their future prospects in the Army – or the lack thereof!

At the end of his visit, the General Officer Commanding (GOC) in Aden laid on a dinner party at Flagstaff House to which he invited a number of senior Officers serving in the Aden Brigade who had worked with his distinguished visitor over the years. Probably the most junior of the group was the Second in Command of 1 PARA, who had been a cadet at Sandhurst when the MS had been a College Commander.

The group duly assembled at the GOC's residence for pre-dinner drinks in friendly mood – they were all professional soldiers and most were known to each other, when into this rather monastic gathering was injected Tony and Madame Hesse. Tony was a merchant venturer, half French-half Arab, who had chosen to remain in Aden after the British departure. His particular skill, as he was the first to admit, was to cheat people in seven languages. What was particular about Tony was not his entrepreneurial reputation but his wife. Madame Hesse was all French – and all woman. To a bunch of soldiers who had not seen a white woman for six months (apart from the Matron at the RAF Hospital who looked as if she'd gone ten rounds with Henry

Cooper and come off worst), Madame was something quite unreal, particularly in what was then the heyday of the mini-skirt – and hers appeared to barely cover her armpits. Even the Chief Padre (who served to become the Chaplain General, no less) was looking distinctly interested.

However, the GOC, always the perfect diplomat, eventually coaxed everyone into Dinner where Madame, as the sole lady present, occupied the place of honour between the GOC and the MS. About half way through the meal Madame realised that the GOC was talking military shop to his right and the MS was engaged in an equally technical conversation to his left. No one was talking to her – which was not one bit to her liking. She plucked the sleeve of the MS and said, 'Mon General, when I come through your Check Point in my Rolls there is a particular Scottish Sergeant who looks through my window and says 'For F..k sake, screw that' – General, what does he mean?' (As if she didn't know.)

As a conversation stopper, it was a blockbuster. The MS, who was a gentleman of the old school, indicated that the GOC might care to explain and who quickly side stepped it to his Chief of Staff, and so on down the chain. (The Chief Padre at this point was observed to be trying to hide under the table.)

There was no further general conversation – all eyes were on Madame Hesse, who went on to regale the assembled company with an account of how she had been sunbathing naked on her private beach when a helicopter full of soldiers came to hover just above her. She had apparently to wrap her hair band round her crotch before running for cover – and so it went on, but as an object lesson on how to become the centre of attraction it was superb – hence the title.

PADRES ARE A MIXED BLESSING

The Padre of 1 PARA during the final phase of the withdrawal from Aden was an energetic and active officer who believed that his place was where the troops were. They responded to this and his primitive chapel, in an old Arab hut, was filled to overflowing every Sunday by those who were not actually deployed on operations. (It is always noticeable that attendance at Divine Service improves as the risk of being killed increases – and decreases when the pressure is off.)

On one occasion, the Padre was accompanying the Second-in-Command on a visit to a forward Company when a shoot-out started and the party was obliged to take cover. Padres do not bear arms under the Geneva Convention but on this occasion someone had given the Padre a grenade and pulled the pin. He crawled up alongside the Second-in-Command, who was busy directing fire on to the terrorists, carrying his grenade. 'What shall I do with this? he asked. The answer was not recordable but happily he had played cricket in his youth and scored a good hit on an enemy firing position.

Nonetheless, the Second-in-Command made a mental note to confine the Padre to more pastoral duties in the future.

"It's only a suggestion, but let's not forget
who's making it."

It was firmly believed that the remaining British Battalions would form a tight perimeter round Khormaksar airfield and the Port area until the time came (still several months hence) for the final pull out, once the British Forces 'up country' had withdrawn.

One of the side effects of this was that 1 PARA could evacuate the tented Radfan Camp, if you could call the fly-blown patch of desert a camp, and base themselves in what they firmly believed was the lap of air conditioned luxury on the RAF section of Khormaksar airfield. When the word came down from on high that 1 PARA were to remain in Radfan Camp for the rest of the operation, the toms were not amused, more particularly since another British Battalion, the South Wales Borderers, had been moved into the Ma'ala Straight to occupy former married quarters left empty by the evacuation of the remaining service families and dependants to the UK.

The thought of the SWB living in luxury while 1 PARA, who had the sharpest of sharp-end operational roles, as befits a Parachute Battalion, was particularly galling.

One morning the Second-in-Command, carrying out a routine check of the perimeter defences, noticed that several of the dug-in tents had a fridge. On checking further it became apparent that every single tent had its own private fridge – a valuable asset when chocolate bars and even boot polish liquified in the intense heat. Clearly, thought the Second-in-Command, these fridges had not been obtained by fair means and hence he sought out the RSM to investigate, a standard procedure when it may be necessary to disown or perhaps not become officially aware of the outcome.

The RSM cracked it in less than an hour. Every RSM has its own intelligence network of key personnel to whom he turns in times of need. This time it was the Sanitary Corporal. He later reported his findings to the Second-in-Command. 'It was like this Sir,' he started echoing the Sanitary Corporal's words verbatim. 'We saw those SWBs living it up in the Ma'ala Straight so we got three trucks, half a dozen men and a millboard and called on each of the former married quarters in turn. We've come to collect your fridge for backloading to the supply depot. It's number 7644321, isn't it? No, said the bemused residents, ours is 1234567. Oh, that's right, it's here on the next page. (This last accompanied a flurry of pages on the millboard.) OK chaps – load it on the truck. We got enough for every tent before we were tumbled and even had two over, which we sold to the charwallah!'

There are times when senior officers should not take too close an interest in how their unit functions. This was one of them. The SWB never forgave 1 PARA but they were withdrawn to the UK after a few weeks where, sadly, they formed part of an amalgamation with the Welsh Regiment.

This may have proved a blessing in disguise since inter-regimental enmities persist long after the original participants have departed.

★

It is sometimes difficult not to interfere in the affairs of others. After the NLF (National Liberation Front), who were Marxist, sponsored by the USSR, had secured their victory over FLOSY (Front for the Liberation of Occupied South Yemen), Moslem Fundamentalists, who were sponsored by Egypt, there was an orgy of blood letting.

It was tragic to see truckloads of ashen faced FLOSY supporters being taken north into the desert (and hence outside the area still controlled by the British) and to hear the long bursts of machine gun fire as they were executed by the NLF. A clandestine patrol from 1 PARA launched from Dar Said reported mass graves being dug up by some scavenging dogs who fed on the corpses.

Our orders were crystal clear; 'It's not our problem. Don't get involved.' Sometimes it's difficult to obey orders.

SARGE WHAT AM I LOOKING FOR?

8

Training the Next Generation

The Parachute Regiment Battle School at Brecon ran such comprehensive courses for Senior NCOs that the concept was expanded to embrace the whole of the Infantry and the Unit re-designated as the NCOs Tactics Wing of the School of Infantry. A spin-off was a most welcome increase in permanent staff, which previously had been provided, with great difficulty, by the Parachute Battalions.

Sadly, those who appeared to fill these slots (or not fill them since some went absent en route) were not always the best soldiers in their regiments. One can imagine the scene in the Company Office. 'Sarn't Major, we have to send a LCpl as a storeman to some place called Brecon, wherever that is. Who can we spare?' the Company Commander would ask. 'Ah Sir, I have just the man in mind, LCpl X, he has a large debtor balance, is quite useless, has three wives and a problem. Let's send him Sir.'

The drill when this sorry crew appeared at the Battle School involved an early interview with the CO. 'I didn't want to come here Sir, and I don't want to stay. I request to be sent back to my Battalion as soon as possible,' was the usual opening gambit. The CO would look wise and say he would re-consider this request in a fortnight.

It so happens that there is an element of free love in Brecon, from which all the boys emigrate to Bristol or London to seek their fortunes, leaving all the girls behind. It was unusual for a newly-arrived soldier not to have his feet under someone's table within days. When he had his next interview he was liable to say, 'Sir, I've changed my mind. I'd quite like to stay on.' Then the CO knew he'd got a motivated soldier.

Thereafter he always had the ultimate sanction against misdemeanours. 'Any more nonsense like this and it's straight

65

back to your Battalion!' This did the trick beautifully and the School had the lowest level of military offences in the whole of Western Command.

CAN A BLACK MAN BLUSH?

The Commanding Officer of the Parachute Regiment Battle School at Brecon served two masters; the Regimental Colonel for the Parachute Regiment Recruit and Juniors NCOs Courses and the Commandant of the School of Infantry for the Senior NCOs Course, which trained potential Platoon Sergeants on an infantry-wide basis. Nonetheless, he was a happy Officer. One of his bosses was based at Aldershot, 120 miles away, and the other at Warminster, 80 miles distant; thanks to his 'moles' on their staffs, neither could arrive unannounced.

One winter's day, when the makee-learnee Platoon Sergeants were digging in on Concrete Hill, arguably the most bleak terrain in the whole of South Wales, for the Defence Exercise which formed the climax of the course, a phone call was received from the School of Infantry to the effect that the Commandant, a distinguished Brigadier, would be visiting the course at noon by helicopter. He would be bringing a guest in the form of a Nigerian Major General, whose country had just emerged from a disastrous civil war. Nigeria intended to form its own Infantry School, of which he was to be the Commandant, based on the British model.

The Commanding Officer took one look at the sky, which was black and lowering, the 40 knot wind and rain coming down like stair rods, and decided 'No Chance' of a helicopter reaching Concrete Hill. He went straight back to supervising the exercise.

Incredibly, right on 12 o'clock, the beat of an approaching helicopter became apparent, heading for Concrete Hill. The Commanding Officer, muttering imprecations under his breath, made it back to the Landing Zone in no time flat, having run cross country for Sandhurst in his youth.

He made it with seconds to spare as a helicopter, badly buffetted by the strong wind, set itself down rather gingerly on the old concrete airstrip, which gave the hill its name. Out of it emerged the Brigadier of the School of Infantry dressed, as was his wont, in combat kit, together with a Nigerian Officer dressed in full fig; Service Dress uniform, Sam Browne Belt, highly polished shoes, gold leafed cap with its red general's band.

Braving the rain and wind, this apparition rushed over to the Commanding Officer, still standing stiffly at the salute, and embraced him warmly shouting above the gale, 'Don't you remember me?' The Commanding Officer, who was no more colour prejudiced than the next man, but who was not accustomed to black generals, however distinguished, falling on his neck, brushed him off with a remark to the effect that no he didn't since you black men all look alike to me. This produced a voluble response from the beautifully dressed Nigerian General, 'When you were an instructor at the Skill at Arms Wing, I was one of your Students. You were a Captain and I was a 2nd Lieutenant. Now I'm a General and you're only a Lieutenant Colonel. Aren't I lucky! Ha, Ha, Ha!'

This little speech endeared him no end to the Commanding Officer, who, nonetheless, clicked straight back into military protocol and appreciated that his guest was hardly dressed for the semi-arctic climate of South Wales in the depth of winter.

Running the logistic back-up for the exercise, based on the edge of the helicopter landing pad, was a small team of cooks and bottle washers under a well-known regimental character, Colour Sergeant 'Dad' Streetday, so named because of the number of his children.

Above the gale, the Commanding Officer shouted to him, 'Colour Sarnt. The Nigerian General is hardly dressed for this weather. Can you find him a pair of gumboots?' The Colour Sergeant, who had spent a lifetime fighting various sorts and conditions of blackmen in many anti-terrorist campaigns and whose prejudice was nothing if not positive, roared back, 'No, let the Black Bastard take his shoes off and pad around in his bare feet, like he does in his own country.'

Of the Colour Sergeant's many sterling qualities, speaking softly in a force 8 gale was not one of them and his words were heard by all concerned. (Now go back to the title.)

The NCOs Tactics Wing at Brecon was called upon, every Easter, to host a number of Combined Cadet Force units from a wide variety of schools who wished to carry out adventurous training in the Beacons. Most of these were led by get-up-and-go Schoolmaster Officers who were keen to get the best deal for their cadets in terms of challenge, endurance and variety of expedition. Some, however, which quickly became apparent, were content to launch their cadets forth on to the mountains, then sit in the mess drinking coffee (or whatever) until the time came to go and pick them up at the end of their trek. Inevitably it was one of these that lost a cadet and pressed the panic button just as the staff of the NCOs Wing was about to depart for their Easter break. All leave was stopped, search parties organised and a mountain rescue team summoned from RAF Valley in Anglesey; a group of underwater experts was even detailed to search the canal in case the unfortunate cadet had drowned.

It transpired after 48 hours of fruitless and frustrating effort that the cadet in question had become bored with the low level of activity laid on by his laid-back officers and had hitched a lift to Birmingham where he was shacked up with his girlfriend (he was one of the more mature cadets!). Only with difficulty were the staff of the NCOs Wing precluded from lynching the officers of that particular cadet unit. At least they never asked to come again!

The Instructors at the Tactics Wing also had a simple system of ensuring that the major exercise which formed the climax of the course went well.

The slowest (and frequently the most portly) of the overseas students was selected to be the Armoured Squadron Commander for the Exercise; nominally the command of an Armoured Combat Team being the greatest honour. In practice, the Corporal tank crewman who was the Squadron Senior Radio Operator commanded the Combat Team. 'Here Sir, have a cup of coffee and leave everything to us,' he would say, having previously secreted a liberal supply of Thermos flasks around the tank turret in place of shell cases – then, to the Squadron over the radio, 'All Stations this is TANGO ONE. Same positions as on the last exercise – GO!' No wonder the overseas student's final report read as if he walked on water!

9

North o' the Border

15 PARA were proud of their secondary title of SCOTTISH VOLUNTEERS, which represented their history as the only geniunely Scots unit to survive in Airborne Forces. They had a long tradition of producing Commanding Officers from amongst their own ranks and had always been resistant to the idea of a Regular.

The big bang in TA terms came in 1967, when both the Regular and Territorial Armies were brought into a single operational Order of Battle under the 'one Army Concept' – largely driven by the need for economies in the Defence Budget but tailored to meet the needs of the NATO Alliance with considerable finesse.

A spin-off from this major upheaval was that the TA Parachute Battalions were given a role in BAOR which involved frequent visits to Germany for recces, conferences and exercises; no easy task for a TA Officer with a civilian career in parallel with his military activities.

This period coincided, by pure chance, with a dearth of credible candidates for command among the TA Officers of 15 PARA and hence, somewhat reluctantly, they were prevailed upon to accept a Regular Officer as CO. Their one stipulation was that he should be an Englishman. The Battalion had companies in both the Highlands and the Lowlands and a Scot, they felt, was sure to be partizan for one or the other.

Thus it was that the new regular CO, who had seldom been North of the Border, was faced with the problem of not having a common language with his Command, particularly in Glasgow where they spoke a patois not known to the rest of the human race. He spent his first few months saying, with great deliberation, 'I do not under-stand your problem. Please speak more slow-ly.' The climax to his introduction to the Battalion came at the first Dinner

Night, at which the Pipe Major, as is the custom in Scottish Regiments, marched round the table making indescribable sounds on his 'agony bags'. Finally, he stopped behind the CO's chair and quoth 'Werrr wan ye tae select ah toon.' After a few repetitions it became clear to the CO that he was being invited to choose the next musical rendering. This was not his field. 'Er-Er-How about Highland Laddie?' he muttered. Wrong 'Och,' said the Pipe Major, 'thas a Campbell toon – we dinna play Campbell toons in this B'tallion.' Clearly the CO had to try again. 'Well, how about Scotland the Brave?' Wrong again. 'Och,' said the Pipe Major, 'ah jest playd that. Did ye no reckonise it? (No!) At this point the CO gave up. 'Play any bloody thing you like, Pipe Major,' he said and returned, with some relief, to his substantial dram which COs are expected to drink at frequent intervals.

Who said only the Americans and the English were divided by a common language?

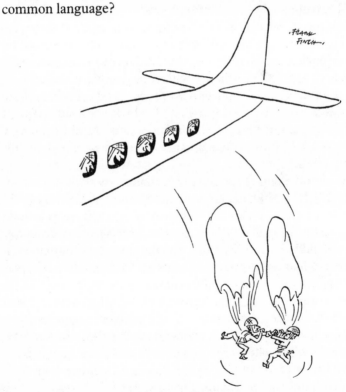

"'Step outside,' he said, 'and say that again.'"

The Andover Squadron based at RAF Thorney Island deployed to RAF Macrihanish for a week or so each autumn to carry out intensive low-level sorties in the highlands, combined with a series of para drops.

15 PARA were invited to mobilise their permanent Staff, the Glaswegian unemployed and any others available, to provide the parachutists. As a sweetener, the CO of the Andover Squadron agreed to produce all his aircraft to drop the bulk of 15 PARA on the Friday night at Barry Budden at the start of an exercise which was already in the programme, mounting from RAF Turnhouse.

It so happened that the Friday evening selected was the date chosen to celebrate the Battle of Britain and the resident RAF at Turnhouse were conspicuous by their absence (socialising) when 15 PARA assembled to mount the drop.

It transpired also that the civilian fire crews, without whom the airfield could not operate, were on a lightning strike in pursuit of the redress of some grievance but were returning to their duties at midnight. Hurried telephone conversations with the Andover Squadron CO at Macrihanish re-established the exercise, with a pick up at 0030 to drop the first lift at 0100 and the second at 0130 hrs. The Training Major had by this time sought out the CO at RAF Turnhouse, who, having by then drink taken, was delighted to invite 15 PARA to join in their Battle of Britain celebrations for an hour or two, combat kit and collywobbles notwithstanding.

While the Battalion repaired to the various RAF Messes, the CO tried to contact the DZ Safety Officer, who was already established at Barry Budden. After trying the DZ extension, then the camp, without success, he sought advice from the RAF Parachute Jumping Instructor, who was wise in the ways of his boss. 'Try the Bruce Hotel at Carnoustie,' he suggested. So the CO did, eventually being put through to the Manageress. 'I wish to speak to Flight Lieutenant X,' he said. 'Och, that's a wee bitty deeficult,' she replied, 'he's in bed with the barmaid just now! Has the drop been cancelled?' 'No,' said the CO, 'postponed.' 'Och,' said the lady again, 'if ye gie me the revised P Hours, when he's finished duin', what he's duin', I'll see he gets the worrd!' The CO gave the new timings for the first and second lifts when the lady

71

said, 'I want to get this quite right. Are these ALPHA timings or ZULU timings?' Good on you, thought the CO. You train 'em well!

Later the drop took place exactly on time but the CO was concerned at the effect of the excitement of the descent and the very chilly night air on the troops, who had imbibed freely of the RAF's kind hospitality, since a DZ casualty or two on a night descent is not unusual.

'You won't believe this,' said the Adjutant, having got his RV report, 'they're all here and they're all fit – but they're all p----d! Knowing the value of discretion, 15 PARA went on to minimum stags till first light. The moral would appear to be that night drops don't hurt if you're well oiled.

'I can't get it out – its stuck and I daren't let go of the bomb!'

15 PARA were grouped with 4th Canadian Mechanised Brigade Group, which had already been reinforced by a German Panzer Battalion of Leopard Tanks, to represent a Soviet surprise attack from across the Iron Curtain.

The Canadian Commander, a Brigadier General, decided to seize the initiative, as the Soviets would, by starting his attack 6 hours early, so 15 PARA were dropped in Company Groups at last light instead of midnight, to seize those well-known choke points, the Springge Gap, the Rodenberg Gap and the Coppenbrugge complex.

Major Pete Berry found himself commanding HQ Company, which had been instantly re-roled as a mini-rifle company for exercise purposes.

Having dropped at Rodenberg and melted into the forest, his group came across a whole Squadron of British tanks in a hide area, snuggled down for a few hours sleep before the start of the exercise. These were promptly captured and marked with the numerals XV in maroon aerosol spray, which all members of 15 PARA were carrying. All the tank officers were away at an O Group except for one very young 2nd Lieutenant, who popped out of his turret, refusing to believe his whole Squadron had been captured by what appeared to be a bunch of bandits in combat caps.

'I demand to see an officer,' quoth he. Pete Berry appeared, his craggy face blacked up for night ops, and, with the peak of his cap pointing slightly off to starboard and the point of his nose slightly off to port, he must have presented a fearsome sight. 'I am a f...ing officer,' he replied and slammed the turret lid down on the young man's fingers. The cavalry officer retired hurt to the depths of his mechanical monster to ponder whether fingers grow again and there was not a bit of trouble from the captured tank Squadron from then on.

All the other elements of 15 PARA had similar success and after 24 hours the exercise had completely bogged down with a large part of the covering force captured or knocked out. The Corps Commander, General Tubby Butler (of happy memory), blew the whistle and ordered both sides back 40 kms to start the exercise again at first light the next day. CO 15 PARA was summoned to the Canadian Brigadier General's 'O' Group, which gave effect to this decision.

All the COs were assembled in the customary semi circle with the German Panzer Battalion Commander and PARA Battalion CO on the flanks. 'These f...ing English,' said the General by way of introduction, 'have made me go back 40 clicks.' (At this point the Panzer Battalion Commander, who had fought in the desert, was nodding vigorously and saying 'Ja, Ja, f...ing English.')

Suddenly the General became aware that the CO of his Parachute Battalion was one of those same f...ing English and looked slightly disconcerted. 'Not to worry General,' said CO 15 PARA, 'I command a Scottish Battalion and we've been fighting the f...ing English on and off for over 2,000 years!' Diplomacy triumphed and the O Group proceeded.

The final phase of the exercise provided a substantial helicopter force to the Canadian Commander and he decided to fly 15 PARA to LZs behind the Teutoberger Wald by tactical routes to disrupt the enemy rear area before linking up with his advancing armour.

This involved splitting the Battalion into half company groups each operating independently. This proved an enormous success and great was the confusion caused. The CO led a group from HQ Company, which, having knocked out an armoured workshop site, captured a tank transporter which had just off-loaded its vehicle casualty. The driver, having been given the option of being notionally killed or of changing sides, decided to stick with his vehicle and off went the transporter with two platoons of 15 PARA on the back and the CO in the cab trying to navigate from an AA book, the Battalion having out run its maps, as is not unusual in fast moving operations.

After 'destroying' an Artillery re-supply column, the tank transporter paused at a T junction while the CO tried to work out which way to turn, when the whole force suddenly jumped off the back and rushed into the Gast Haus. 'My God, discipline has broken down at last,' thought the CO, but he was wrong. What the soldiers could see from their higher viewpoint, which he couldn't, was over a high wall. The entire echelon of 1 GORDONS were pausing for 'refreshment' on their way to resupply their Battalion. The GORDONS QM, all his Colour Sergeants and assorted hangers on were led into captivity while the tank transporter continued its depredations across the rear areas.

The rumours of 15 PARA's progress began to reach Corps HQ, since other groups had also equipped themselves with transport, and, as usual, these had become exaggerated as they were passed up the chain of command. At one point the Parachute Brigade Major, who was acting as the PARA LO at Exercise Control, was dispatched by a senior staff officer to put CO 15 PARA under close arrest. The Brigade Major, who had seen the effect of PARA forces injected into rear areas before, wisely retired to a Gast Haus to monitor the Corps Command Net. Eventually he located General Tubby's Rover Group and put the matter to him. 'Just what I would have done had I been the CO,' said Tubby, and the heat when straight out of the situation. Such is the power of command!

OPERATION PERISHER

The Royal Navy run a training course for makee-learnee submarine captains at Faslane, which was originally styled a 'Periscope Course' but over the years has become corrupted to a 'Perisher' Course. One of the evolutions a trainee captain has to perform successfully is the launching of a small raiding force from the sea in darkness and their recovery on the following night. The Royal Marine Commando at Arbroath normally provided this but in the autumn of 1970 they were playing an away match on the streets of the Ardoyne and were definitely not available. 15 PARA were asked to fill the gap.

The concept involved the raiding party of 6 assembling in the forward torpedo room with half inflated Geminis. Once the sub surfaced, the party pulled their boats on to the casing and completed their inflation with an airline from below. The boats then launched and separated to the full extent of 100 m of cable, hanging an EASCO lifejacket light over the rear of each.

The sub then submerged and, using the lights as aiming marks, caught the cable at roughly mid point with its periscope and towed the inflatables inshore. When the depth began to get critical, the sub flashed two greens from its periscope and backed off. The

75

boats then made their way ashore to assassinate the President, blow up an oil well or whatever, and next night put out to sea for the return RV with the submarine.

This is the most hazardous part of the whole operation. Bucking about in even a moderate sea in an inflatable with an EASCO light blinking on the stern, on a black night, peering through a prismatic compass, trying to get sight on different landmarks ashore and hoping you're in roughly the right place is liable to be an uplifting experience. It really makes your day to see the sub's periscope cleaving through the water, catching the line between the boats and towing them out to sea far enough for the raiding party to re-embark safely.

The third invitation to 15 PARA to provide a raiding party came in mid-December for a launch on a Saturday night with the pick up on Sunday. Christmas festivities and Bounty Balls (then in vogue) were in full swing, so rounding up even six volunteers was not easy. Eventually it was settled that the Training Major should command one boat with two TA volunteers and a newly-joined TA Officer the other, with the Battalion's RAF PJI Sergeant and a TA Corporal as his crew.

The launch was a disaster from the start. The sea was particularly rough and the Firth of Clyde, as one might expect in mid-December, was rather more than bloody cold. The trainee sub Captain misjudged his manoeuvre and brought his boat up too far to starboard, actually under the right-hand Gemini. A projection on the casing punctured some of the compartments and the boat began to take water and worse, to jack-knife in the middle. The Standard Procedure for problems, which had been emphasised in the briefing, was for the sub to back off and leave the boats to get ashore as best they could and for the undamaged boat to cut the cable and proceed on its own to carry out the assigned mission. Accordingly, the sub disappeared and the Training Major, having established by shouting that the other boat was still seaworthy, if only just, cut the cable and made for the shore.

The crew of the damaged boat, unable to start the water-logged outboard, started to paddle but the heavy sea and the deteriorating state of the boat made this a slow process. After some time, the officer gave up and announced that 'We're all doomed. We must pray.' Happily, the PJI Sergeant was made of sterner stuff. He knocked out the officer with his paddle and placed his supine body across the front of the boat, which immediately improved its position in the water by levelling out the jack-knife effect. 'F...ing row,' he said to the Corporal, who had been watching this performance goggle-eyed. Between them, they propelled the boat towards the shore, painfully slowly, pausing only to clout the officer with their paddles when he started to come round.

Eventually they landed safely, thanks to their determination and good old fashioned guts, which so often comes to the fore when the chips are really down. The officer was quietly removed from the Battalion, the Corporal was promoted to Sergeant and the PJI awarded the Queen's Commendation for Bravery.

There can't be many RAF Sergeants who have been decorated for hitting an officer. Is this unique?

GET YOURSELF A GOOD LAWYER

15 PARA held a Study Period in the Spring of 1969 and the CO invited a US Army Colonel, then based in London and recently returned from the war in Vietnam, which was then in full swing, to speak on his experiences in combat. The Colonel flew up to Glasgow on the Friday afternoon and the MT Corporal Ingles was dispatched to pick him up in the staff car.

On their return, the Corporal reported to the CO, 'Ahkudna-understandafuckinworrdtheColonelsedSir,' which, after a couple of repetitions, was translatable, while the American Colonel, in his Southern drawl, asked 'Wuz he speaking in English? We were talking but we were definitely not comoonicatin!' Such is the versatility of the common language.

That evening the CO gave a drinks party to introduce the Colonel to locally based Officers and it was immediately apparent, from some secret sign which had obviously passed between them, that the US Army Colonel and the Battalion Quartermaster, were both masons. After a few drams, the QM carried the Colonel off to his home, which was only two streets away, where they apparently talked masonic shop and consumed the best part of a gallon of rum, which he, like all good Quartermasters, had concealed in the boot of his car.

They then returned to the CO's house, where, perhaps unwisely, they imbibed a few more drams. At this point the American Colonel announced that he proposed to have 'a quiet cerebral haemorrhage' and retired to bed. The Quartermaster, made to drive home, overshot his house, hit another car in turning round and quite spoiled the other driver's day. The QM was not disposed to argue the toss and they were descending into fisticuffs when a passing police patrol invited them to blow into the bag.

The next morning the CO was rung by the Giffnock police, who invited him to come and collect a much chastened and definitely hung-over Quartermaster. Later they rang again to say that the normal limit was 70 to 80 milligrams and we might be interested to know that the Quartermaster had recorded 480, which was unusual, even for Glasgow. They were thinking of sending it to the Guiness Book of Records.

A prosecution ensued and advice was sought from OC C Coy, who was himself a writer to the signet. While not being a drink/drive specialist personally, he had a friend who was. 'Go for trial by Jury,' advised this worthy, 'and trust me. I'll get you off but it'll cost you!'

Opting for a Jury Trial delayed the case by 7 months and, when the case came to Court, the Doctor who had examined the Quartermaster had joined the Brain Drain and emigrated to Canada. Only 'best evidence' being admissible, part of the case immediately lapsed. The lawyer then went to town on the two constables and eventually discovered the key. One said it was a fine evening and the other that it was raining, as it usually does on a weekend in Glasgow. (The state of the weather was entirely irrelevant. The Quartermaster was smashed out of his mind.) The summing up for the defence was masterful, 'Gentlemen of the Jury, if these two worthy police officers cannot agree even on the state of the weather, how can you respect their judgement on the evidence before you, etc., etc.?' He established a 'reasonable doubt' and the Quartermaster got off.

The moral would appear to be; never mind the evidence – get yourself a good lawyer.

In 1969, the Adjutant ran recruit and pre-parachute course training for the Battalion.

He spent many hours on the telephone researching the issue of a Fan Trainer to assist in sorting out the men from the boys but, sadly, without success. Then he had a brilliant idea, which he put to the CO. We would write ourselves a back-dated letter of authority for the issue of a fan to all TA units more than a 100 miles from the PTS, purporting to come from the Land/Air Warfare Branch in the MOD and which was then in the process of merging with ASD 12, using the signature block of an officer who had already retired and was, therefore, untouchable, and addressed to HQ Eastern Command, which had been disbanded two years previously. The letter was typed, jumped on a few times to make it look appropriately ancient and photocopied.

The CO then walked the photocopy round HQ Scotland, who not only authorised a Fixed Fan in what is now Pearson Hall, but also a mobile lego land-type fan for training the outlying companies.

The pen may not be mightier than the sword but it's a powerful weapon nonetheless in skilful hands.

THE PERFECT CRIME

In the early seventies, it was announced that the TA would be paid by Giro cheque instead of in cash as before. This was greeted with groans of disapproval since most of TA soldiers had convinced their wives that they weren't paid at all for being in the TA and a few bold spirits had gone so far as to declare that it actually cost them money to join.

It so happened that the final training weekend when cash was to be paid coincided with the departure of a much loved and respected Sergeant Major Permanent Staff Instructor from B Company 15 PARA in Aberdeen. Since the exercise was not due to start until the Saturday morning, the cash for the weekend's pay was drawn from the bank on the Friday and lodged overnight in the company safe ready for parade next day. A farewell party for the Sergeant Major was held on the Friday evening and the Company Office used as a cloakroom – hence virtually everyone had a legitimate reason for being in the office during the course of the evening.

Come the dawn, the pay had gone – every last penny of several thousand pounds.

A check was immediately initiated to see who had keys to the Company safe. It transpired that the safe had been installed by the Highland TAFA when the TA was formed in 1907 and that every member of the permanent Staff since then either had his own key or had had one cut. After identifying 23 keys the Commanding Officer, who was personally investigating the loss, gave up and sent for the Special Investigation Branch (the Army equivalent of the CID). An RMP Sergeant duly appeared and set up a watch to see if any member of the Company bought another car – or another wife – but to no avail. In any event he was whipped off after 48 hours to pursue a Peeping Tom case at Redford Barracks in Edinburgh.

The upshot was that the missing money stayed missing. After a few months and a mountain of paperwork, the Army board issued notice of its displeasure to the Commanding Officer, who was ultimately responsible for everything that happened in 15 PARA, and the Company Commander, who in civil life was a schoolmaster. The CO rang his Company Commander to tell him the sad news. 'Bill,' he said, 'you and I have incurred the severe displeasure of the Army Board.' 'Really,' replied the Company Commander, 'now what about that range allocation I asked for next weekend . . .'

It couldn't have done either of them any harm. The CO retired as a Brigadier and the Company Commander is a most distinguished Headmaster and a most revered member of his local TA Association.

10

Upsets in Ulster

THE AMBUSH THAT NEVER WAS

The Headquarters of the 3rd Infantry Brigade, during the early seventies, was based in a disused industrial building at Lurgan known to the soldiers as the 'Knicker Factory', due to its previous existence before 'the troubles'.

It was relatively secure having high walls and only two entrances, one of which had been sealed, but being situated on a hill and sticking up like a mini skyscraper, it was an easy target for even the most inaccurate of long-range snipers.

One of these 'try your luck' experts was particularly persistent, always having a go after the pubs closed on a Saturday night. He would only fire a few rounds, most of which hammered harmlessly into the brickwork, and be off before the mobile patrols of the 13/18 Hussars, which operated in the urban area, could pinpoint him.

On one particular Saturday, he got lucky and put two shots through the window of the Brigade Operations Room, which embedded themselves in the plastic mapboard (much to the consternation of the duty intelligence NCO, who fortunately was unhurt). By projecting the line of fire backwards from the spent rounds in the map board to the neat round holes in the window it was possible, by the application of some fairly basic balistics, to pinpoint the area from which the sniper had fired. The Deputy Commander of the Brigade, who had developed a particular grudge against the sniper, disguised himself as a Trooper of the 13/18 Hussars and spent an energetic evening as a member of one of their mobile patrols, concentrating carefully, but not too obviously on the group of five or six terraced houses in a strongly Republican area from which the sniping was thought to have originated.

There was luckily an area of waste ground adjacent to the suspect houses on which had grown up some straggly bushes, just

81

enough to provide cover by night, if not in daylight, for a group of not more than three. The Deputy Commander identified this as a possible ambush site and worked up a minor operation to give the phantom sniper more than he bargained for. The idea, like most military plans, was essentially simple. An ambush group comprising the Deputy Commander and two soldiers with a General Purpose Machine Gun would join a mobile patrol.

Snap Vehicle Check Points were normally only established for five minutes or so and when the vehicle crew remounted to continue their patrol, the ambush group would melt away into the bushes to await the incidence of sniper activity from the suspect houses when he would receive something of a surprise packet. The mobile patrol would remain within fairly close proximity, on call by pocket radio, to provide a back-up or to seal the area as the situation developed. If for some reason the sniper decided not to show, the mobile would recover the ambush group by another VCP during the small hours and well before daylight.

This plan was put to the Brigade Commander for approval. The Brigadier eyed his Deputy with some disdain. Officers of the rank

Just pull the pin and throw it. There's no need
to gift wrap 'em".

of Full Colonel, he expressed himself with some force, were not supposed to lurk in the back streets of Lurgan leading two-man ambush groups. However, since it was necessary to discourage further sniping he allowed himself to be persuaded and the operation went forward. The Deputy Commander picked his pair with some care. The gunner was the champion shot of the Brigade Signal Squadron and his Number 2 was an intelligence NCO with a good grasp of the local dialect, having himself been born in Belfast; a useful asset if for some reason words had to be exchanged.

The group went through the operation on the map, on a rough model of the ground and all had the chance to view the proposed scene of possible combat in daylight by accompanying one of the 13/18 Hussars mobile patrols. They also practised emergency drills for calling up support if one or more became casualties.

Finally, they all check-zeroed their weapons by day and their individual weapon sight on the machine gun (known colloquially as the Starlight scope) by night, firing from and through bushes similar to those on the waste ground. Seldom can an ambush have been better prepared.

By ten o'clock on the next Saturday night the ambush group had been dropped off and were in position awaiting events. During the next hour several groups of locals returned to the houses under observation, most of whom had, as they say, drink taken. By about eleven, when the sniper could be expected to have a go at the Knicker Factory, the ambush group were as taut as bow strings with that pre-action sinking feeling and what felt like gallons of adrenalin pumping round their blood streams.

What did happen was almost beyond belief. Instead of sniper fire, one of the houses literally erupted like a volcano and bits fell in all directions showering the ambush group with debris. The houses on either side looked in imminent danger of collapse and one immediately took fire. The ambush group summoned the mobile, which was on its way in any event, since it could hardly ignore an explosion of that magnitude, and the combined force was able to control the locals, who appeared anxious to remove items from the shattered building, and to start the evacuation of the nearby houses until the RUC and the Fire Brigade arrived and took over. The locals may have been puzzled to see one elderly trooper and two more with a machine gun clearly camouflaged for covert action in their midst but the pressures of the moment were such that it passed unnoticed, or at least unremarked.

The Ammunition Technical Officer, who investigated the incident, found bits of no less than three terrorists who had clearly scored an 'own goal'. Bombs, particularly large ones, which this apparently was, require handling with care. Perhaps after a night on the bevvy one of them had got careless as they started to prepare their bomb, presumably to blow a hole in the wall of the factory. No one will ever know their intentions but from the balance of bomb making equipment found in the ruins, it was obvious that they were not new to the art.

The ambush group never got their chance with the phantom sniper but he must have been one of the casualties from the explosion since the Saturday night episodes ceased thereafter.

The ambush that never was . . . Well, you can't win them all!

"Oh dear, I think you've hit the bull!"

The operational situation in Northern Ireland in the early seventies had reached what the politicians called an 'acceptable level of violence' (whatever that means) and some degree of normality was returning to the civic life of the Province.

May is the traditional time for the changeover of Mayors and other civic dignatories and on this occasion the local Brigadier was invited to attend the ceremony of Mayor Making in Lurgan. The Brigadier quickly and quite legitimately pleaded pressure of work in South Armagh, where the terrorist threat was still temporarily in the ascendant, and detailed his Deputy, to attend in his place.

It was a plain clothes affair and the Colonel, being an old hand in matters terrorist, took the sensible precaution of slipping his Browning automatic pistol into the waistband of his smart city suit before joining the new Mayor and Corporation at the Cathedral to pray for a degree of success during their year of office.

The congregation, like the animals in the Ark, marched up the aisle two by two, the Colonel being paired off with the local Bishop. Halfway to their appointed seats it became clear that the Browning pistol had detached itself from the Colonel's waistband and was working its way down his trouser leg. Begging the Bishop to pause briefly be retrieved it from his ankle and replaced it in his belt but, sadly, it appeared to the Bishop that, during its short transit, the pistol was pointing straight up his left nostril. Thinking he was about to be assassinated by the strange person in plain clothes by his side, he threw his episcopal crook to the ground and called upon the Virgin and the Saints. This contretemps was sorted out relatively quickly and after a prayer or two the congregation repaired to the Mayor's Parlour where the serious business of the ceremony, the drinking, was to be conducted.

After the old Bushmills Whiskey had circulated a few times, one of the Councillors staggered up to the Colonel and said in an Irish accent you could cut with a knife, 'Hey youse. Did youse say y're name was Star-lin?' On receiving an affirmative reply, he went on, 'In that case, ye must be related to the Tim Star-lin of the Province?' Again an affirmative reply as he was a distant cousin. 'In that case youse must also be related to the John Star-lin that murdered the Roman Catholic Archbishop of Colchester in 1381, the year of the Peasants' Revolt' said as a statement of fact; then to the assembly at large, 'Hey. He's wun of uss. His kinsman murdered a Roman Catholic Archbishop; guv 'im another Whiskey!'

That the Colonel was a senior officer in the British Army apparently counted for little, while the fact that a distant ancestor was an East Anglian Bandit in the fourteenth century meant everything. Protestantism hadn't actually been invented at that time – Martin Luther had yet to do his thing! – but memories, or perhaps legends, are the currency of the folklore in Ulster. No wonder the Irish problem continues to be insoluble.

Well *Private Harper* – If your name's on it...that's it.

"Do you think they've seen us?"

86

11

Running an Unconventional Regiment

A Parachute Assault Exercise was held on Salisbury Plain in the mid-seventies with the Regimental Colonel of the Parachute Regiment acting as Chief Umpire.

Due to the demands of operations in Northern Ireland at that time, only two Parachute Battalions were available for the exercise, so the Brigade Commander sought to create a third ad hoc Battalion by inviting companies to join the exercise from the French and German Army Airborne Forces. These, together with the Guards Parachute Company, were formed into an International Battalion, which became known, perhaps inevitably, as the Foreign Legion.

The first phase of the exercise involved the capture of a built-up area. The German Company were slow, methodical and highly professional in their manoeuvre to capture the Southern half of the area. The French arrived, at the trot, without apparently any form of reconnaissance. The Capitaine pointed to the enemy, made mention of national honour and set off again at the run with his Company following in no sort of order. Quelle vitesse, Quelle elan – (but what casualties they would have sustained). We all do things differently!

The final phase of the exercise involved a counter-attack and it was necessary for one of the companies of the Foreign Legion to be notionally driven off its defensive position to provide the trigger for this manoeuvre.

The Chief Umpire approached the Company Commander of the German Company, which was the most exposed tactically. 'Ze French – Zey are withdrawing alzo?' asked the Company Commander. 'Er – No.' 'Zo, in zat case the Gairmans remain hier.'

The Chief Umpire, appreciating national susceptibilities, knew when it was time to back off. He went to visit the French Company instead and invited them to withdraw. 'Are the Germans also withdrawing?' asked the Capitaine. 'Er – No,' replied the Chief Umpire. 'Alors, ils ne passeront pas,' spake the Capitaine, quoting directy from the defence of the Marne in October 1914. 'Au revoir, Monsieur.'

The Chief Umpire realised he had a problem, so he turned, in desperation, to the Guards Parachute Company, inviting them to withdraw. 'But our position is the least exposed of all,' said the Company Commander, 'Why us?'

The time for discussion had long past. The Chief Umpire pointed to the Colonel's badges on his shoulder strap and to the Major's Crown on the Company Commander's. He took the point at once and withdrew his Company. The subsequent counter-attack was a great success.

Rank always has the privilege.

NEVER UNDER-ESTIMATE THE AFRICAN

One of the unusual features of the International Exercise was the presence of a delegation from the Sudan. Their modest Airborne Forces wished to purchase more modern aircraft than the Dakota cast off by the RAF after WWII, and a team, led by an enormous full Colonel, was dispatched to the UK to explore options.

Part of their programme involved a visit to 16 Parachute Brigade which, as it happened, was involved in a major exercise. The Regimental Colonel, acting as Chief Umpire, was 'volunteered' by the Brigade Commander to look after this team, which also involved giving them dinner at home following the post-exercise cocktail party in the Brigade Mess. The two Colonels had met years before when the Sudanese were doing their parachute training at RAF Abingdon and the Regimental Colonel tried to make polite conversation by asking after the other Sudanese Officers who had been on the same course. 'What happened to the group leader, Capt Ahmed?' he asked in all innocence. 'He wuz executed last year', replied the Sudanese Colonel. 'Oh, and what about that Lieutenant who spoke such good English?' asked the Regimental Colonel. 'He wuz executed this year' was the reply. This was a real conversation stopper, so everyone had another large whisky. At this point the family Beagle entered on the look-out for some droppings from the cocktail eats. 'Ah,' said the Sudanese Colonel, 'in my country we would eat a dog as fat as that', which endeared him no end to the Colonel's wife! He then went to the loo and passed out cold, having imbibed freely both at the Brigade Cocktail Party and thereafter.

With some difficulty, as a form of rigor mortis appeared to have seized him, he was manhandled into a Staff car by the other Sudanese, none of whom apparently had the power of speech and no doubt mindful of the fate of the Airborne Officers who were executed. A phone call was made to warn the Brigade Mess to have a bearer party on hand to put the Sudanese Colonel to bed, but apparently his powers of recovery were remarkable. In the fifteeen minutes or so it took to drive back he not only came to but insisted that the Bearer Party join him at the bar, where he kept them up till the small hours (now go back to the title).

GET MARRIED OR ELSE!

The Parachute Regiment values highly its links with the Airborne Forces of our principal allies; links forged largely during the great Airborne Operations of WWII.

A significant element of this bond of friendship is the exchange of officers and NCOs between Airborne Forces; for example the Parachute Regiment always has an officer serving with the US 82nd Airborne Division at Fort Bragg, an officer with the French Airborne School at Pau and another with the Canadian Airborne Regiment at Rivers, Manitoba.

On one occasion, the officer with the Canadians was due to turn over and the Regimental Colonel received a phone call from his opposite number who commanded the Canadian Airborne Regiment. The fact that the conversation took place at 0400 hrs due to the time difference between Canada and the UK and that it was conducted in French did not improve the Regimental Colonel's equilibrium but after a bit he gathered that his Canadian counterpart was not happy with the new nomination for the exchange appointment. 'All our officers are graduates and by the time they join us they are married. Your new guy is single. It won't do. Either change him or get him married – fast,' was the request.

The Regiment Colonel pondered the problem over breakfast and then sent for the young officer concerned, asking how he felt about his proposed posting to Canada. 'Great,' said the young man, 'I'll work with another Airborne Force, see something of Canada and the Canadian Army – and be a Captain two years before my due time. I couldn't be more delighted.' 'Ah,' said the Regimental Colonel, 'there's a slight catch, you've got to be married – by Saturday!'

The young officer saluted and left the Colonel's office, deep in thought. He was back by midday. 'Come to my wedding, Sir?' he said 'on Friday!' At the reception the Colonel sidled up to the bride and asked if all was well. 'I thought he'd never ask,' was all she said.

Subsequently the young officer's tour in Canada was a great success. He is now a senior officer with two lovely children and a rock solid marriage. Talk about the wheel of fortune!

PARACHUTING – CONTINENTAL STYLE

The Regimental Colonel of the Parachute Regiment tries to visit all the countries which have one of his officers on an exchange posting.

Visiting the French Parachute School at Pau high in the Pyrenees, the Regimental Colonel was invited to jump, a standard procedure of all parachute schools to entertain visitors.

The Para Liaison Officer and the Colonel duly appeared to draw and fit 'chutes together with what appeared initially to be about several hundred others from all three services, since the French put all their officers through the parachute course as part of their character development programme.

The LO and the Colonel were detailed to jump from a Transall, very similar to a C130 Hercules but with two not four engines. The load capacity was alleged to be 60 but a rough count indicated over a hundred lining up to get on board. A group of French Army Pathfinders on a free fall course squatted on the ramp looking disdainfully at the mere static line jumpers and talking exclusively among themselves; a course of fifty odd Air Force Officer candidates with their Instructors filled most of the seats in the freight bay, while a makee-learnee jumpmaster course was crammed up against the forward bulkhead and overflowing on to the flight deck. The gaps between the seats, which on a British aircraft would have been left clear, were stuffed with the administration element from the staff of the school. It just happened to be Wednesday and the LO explained that Wednesday afternoons were given over to sport, of which parachuting was by far the most popular, particularly with the administrative staff who spent their days pushing paper, issuing stores or driving trucks. Into this mêlée the Regimental Colonel and the Para LO were shoehorned, feeling rather like passengers in a Japanese subway train.

As a VIP visitor, the Colonel was allowed to jump first, which he was delighted to do, having stood from take off to the Drop Zone in close proximity to an enormous Sergeant-Chef from the Quartermaster's Dept, whose BO was overpowering even with the inherent paraffin smell of turbo assisted aero-engines, and a petite and very attractive lady Sergeant Clerk, as the French train all their school staff to parachute irrespective of sex and employment.

When he finally got outside, the Colonel, on checking his canopy, was horrified to see the lady Sergeant Clerk a few feet above him, having come through his rigging lines in the slipstream and looking for all the world like a bird in a cage of nylon cord. Not a bit put out by this close encounter with a strange visitor, the lady pulled down hard on her front lift webs and, having gained forward momentum, slid gracefully out of the umbrella of the Colonel's 'chute and disappeared, apparently upwards. This was an optical illusion as being of very slight build she descended much more slowly than thirteen stone paratroopers were wont to do. It was the first (and last) time the Colonel ever became entangled with a French lady!

On a separate visit to the Italian Parachute School at Pisa, the Colonel was privileged to be offered a jump from a Nord-Atlas, a twin boom aircraft which had been the workhorse of the continental armies in the fifties and sixties but was by then being phased out in favour of more modern aircraft.

The Carabinieri Parachute Battalion was providing the parachutists and the Colonel and his 'minder' were grafted on to one of their sticks. The aircraft staggered into the air with its full load but from the obviously agitated state of the air force Flight Engineer, all was not well (the Nord-Atlas is a 'see through' aircraft with the flight crew totally visible from the freight bay). The pilot made a circuit and landed, taxi-ing his plane along the perimeter track of the airfield along which were parked a whole line of Nord-Atlas aircraft in various stages of demolition. Coming up to one of these wrecks the Flight Engineer shouted 'Basta' and seizing a tool box jumped out of the door and ran over to one which still had its engines. After a few minutes he returned with a piece of twisted metal tubing which he proceeded to instal in the port engine. Once he was satisfied he called out 'Avanti' and climbed aboard again.

The flight to the Drop Zone was uneventful and not one of the Carabinieri appeared to think this improvised bit of cannibalisation was at all unusual. Nonetheless, the Colonel was quite pleased when his turn came to jump and he was invited 'Alla Porta – Vai' (to the door – GO!). Different strokes for different folks!

VIVE L'ENTENTE CORDIALE

The most successful company-level parachute operation of WWII is acknowledged as the raid on Bruneval by C Coy 2 PARA.

In the mid-seventies, the French authorities decided to hold a commemorative ceremony and asked that the Wartime Company Commander, now a retired Major General, be invited to participate.

The Regimental Colonel of the Parachute Regiment was invited to arrange the attendance of the General, to provide an armed party in full fig for the main ceremony and a parachuting party to make a symbolic descent on to the original Dropping Zone where the principal ceremony was to take place.

The General was approached to attend. 'Not on your life,' he said. 'F...ing Frogs couldn't organise a p...-up in a brewery.' (He was no Francophile.) 'Anyway, I would only consider going if I were the principal VIP.' This, too, was a problem. Lord Louis Mountbatten had already been nominated to represent the

Sovereign by the Palace Secretariat, who organise such things. This was broken gently to the General.

After several liberal snorts of whisky (being a native of Scotland he seldom drank less than the classic 'dram', three fingers wide) he agreed, reluctantly, to attend. 'But I need a destroyer,' he said, 'Lord Louis is sure to cross the channel by grey funnel line. If he has a destroyer, I want one too!' This, too, required more negotiation – and more whisky – but eventually the General agreed to fly with the parading and ceremonial parties in an RAF Hercules.

The great day duly came – which was the Sunday after Airborne Forces Day, the annual regimental reunion, and not a few of the participants were suffering from a delayed hangover. The troops were at Lyneham in good time for the take off at 1100 hrs but at 1115 there was still no sign of the General. (He had been offered a staff car but had declined wishing to do some business connected with his farm en route.) At almost 1130 the Station Commander, who is present in person when a General Officer is in transit through his Airfield, decided that the aircraft would have to go General or no General.

Happily, while the pilot was warming up his engines, the General appeared in a low-flying Landrover, complete with a large pig in the back. 'Tried to sell the pig but couldn't close the deal', he said, in explanation of being late and, turning to the Station Commander who was standing stiffly at the salute, said, 'Be a good chap and feed the pig while I'm away. Here are the keys.' And with that he boarded the aircraft leaving a perplexed Station Commander with a bunch of keys, a Landrover and a pig snorting volubly over the tailboard.

The flight was uneventful and the pilot managed to catch up the lost time but the wind was strong and sick bags were put to good use in the freight bay. On arrival, it was quite clear that the wind, at 30 knots and gusting, was too strong for the symbolic parachute drop and the Regimental Colonel, who was responsible for the British Contingent, decided that both groups, the ceremonial troops and the parachutists, would motor to the Dropping Zone and all participate in the ceremony. As a token gesture, it was arranged that the Hercules would fly over at drop height at the appointed hour just to make the point that the Bruneval Raid had been a joint Army-Air Operation.

The General was met by a phalanx of voluble French VIPs, who carried him off for a 'repas francais' at some local relais. At the field of the ceremony, the British contingent discovered that they had arrived early, as the French element were still enjoying their Sunday lunch. This was unfortunate, since for reasons of protocol, they had to Present Arms to each French party as they arrived. Not only were these from the French Forces but also from virtually every group of Anciens Combattants from the Pas de Calais to the Loire. By the time that all were assembled, the British Contingent was almost ready to drop (literally). Then came the half-hour wait for the VIPs, almost mandatory in any French ceremony, which never runs to time.

The General had clearly had an excellent lunch and was being formally charming to everyone to whom he was introduced, a bad omen for those who knew him well. The first VIP, a certain Monsieur Hereux, then took the Stand and began what turned out to be a 30 minute 'allocution'. Even to those with a rudimentary grasp of the French idiom, it was quite clear that his speech – and probably the whole ceremony – was a set-up to further his political ambitions as a candidate for Mayor of Le Havre. He several times used passages in passable English, referring repeatedly to the Bruneval Raid as 'that great Anglo-French Operation'. This brought the General out of his post-prandial doze quick enough. He was heard to mutter, entirely audibly, 'Anglo-French Operation, my a... Never saw a F...ing Frog during the whole shooting match', and he relapsed into somnolence. If anyone understood they tactfully pretended not to.

Then came Lord Louis's turn to make an 'allocution', which he started in faultless French. After no more than two or three minutes the microphone went dead and a hush fell on the assembled company. Various signals NCOs of the French Army appeared on the dais and, with the standard techniques of their calling, tapped the speaker, 'Une-deux-tois-quatre. Mon Dieu, cet appareil ne marche plus.' Still silence – and so it remained until someone had the bright idea of ringing the local power station. The electrical engineer, when he was finally run to earth, agreed that he had cut the power to the area. There was to be a parachute drop, he said, and since an overhead cable crossed the Dropping

Zone, he had a written order to cut the power to the area at 1500 hrs and to restore it at 1600 hrs. No, no one had told him that the drop was cancelled and, in any event, without another written order the power would stay off until 4 o'clock.

It was the time for urgent action. Monsieur Hereux himself wrote a counter order on the back of an envelope and a Gendarme was dispatched on a motorcycle at high speed to the power station.

During all this 'Le Musique', as the French called their military band and who had been told to provide incidental music, had gone through their repertoire at least twice and were beginning to droop. No one was more pleased than when the power was eventually restored after some 45 minutes. Lord Louis, player that he was, went on imperturbably with his allocution as if nothing had happened, with the General still muttering audibly in the background, 'F...ing Frogs, couldn't organise a rice pudding.'

Lord Louis was succeeded by Monsieur Yvon Bourge, then Minister of National Defence of the Republic, who held forth at length on a subject which appeared to be entirely unrelated to the occasion. After some minutes, the sound of approaching aircraft was heard, coming up for the symbolic flypast and dead on the original forecast time. 'Mon Dieu,' said someone, 'we forgot to ring the airfield and tell them the ceremony was running 45 minutes late.'

Clearly, it was too late to avert the aircraft and one lumbering RAF Hercules escorted by five French Mirage jet fighters, hove into sight and flew meticulously over the Dropping Zone at 100 knots. The Hercules then turned back to the airfield but the Mirage jets, not comfortable at only 100 knots, switched to after burners and literally stood on their tails in a near vertical climb. The back wash of this hit the audience like a hurricane. Ladies lost their picture hats, old comrades had to hang like grim death on to their drapeaux and worst of all, Monsieur Bourge lost his wig – up to this point it had not been obvious that he needed one – but it blew off and went bowling towards the cliff edge pursued by several of his aides, no doubt with their eye on future promotion. One of these managed to retrieve it and return it to the Minister who put it back on and carried on with his speech as if nothing had happened.

Finally, the ceremony ended and the VIPs dispersed. The

Colonel in charge of the French contingent came over to say that his men had put a crate of beer in the back of each of the two trucks used by the British, which he hoped they would enjoy. Sadly, no one had told the two French national servicemen drivers, who had remained with their vehicles, that the beer was for the British. They viewed its arrival as a gift from the Gods and when the British contingent returned they were well and truly plastered. The French Capitaine and his Sergeant Chef, who were looking after the British contingent, threw these miscreants, who were clearly incapable of driving anything, into the back and climbed into the cabs to drive themselves. This was fine until they came to the steep track up the hill, when they both missed their gears and their enormous 'camions' started to run backwards downhill. Renaults and Citroens were seen running for cover to avoid this inexorable rearward movement but happily it was all sorted out and the troops delivered safely back to the airfield.

The General had been carried off again for dinner with the French and, with the passing of time, the pilot began to look anxiously at his watch. When the General eventually arrived he summoned the pilot and asked him how many troops he had on board and did they have rifles. The pilot, mystified, replied that there were about 60 and yes, they had rifles. 'Good,' said the General, 'let us not go back to Lyneham. Fly instead to Uganda. There's a miscreant called Idi Amin that I wish to depose.' The pilot, who thought he meant it, paled visibly and started mumbling about flight plans and diplomatic clearance. The Regimental Colonel, who knew the General better and realised that there was a problem, summoned the Sergeant Major. 'The General wishes to board the Aircraft', he said, and from nowhere two burly Sergeants appeared and assisted their distinguished War Hero on to the Hercules. All in a day's work for the Parachute Regiment.

SERGEANT MAJORS CAN BE ECCENTRIC TOO

Chalky was a Sergeant Major in a Parachute Battalion and was one of nature's characters, epitomised by his readiness to put a whole Flight of the RAF Regiment straight into the Guard Room when they failed to spring to attention as his Company Commander passed. On another occasion, in Bahrein, when his Company was shooting on the only range, he noticed that the flank safety sentry had fallen asleep; not unusual in the heat of a Gulf afternoon. 'Give me your rifle, boy,' he said to the nearest soldier on the firing point, 'I'll put a shot across his bows.' He may have intended so to do but in the event it went straight through the fleshy part of the sentry's right arm. That took a bit of explaining away!

SIR, THE BUTTS HAVE SAID — 'NOW WE'VE PASTED UP THE WARDEN, IS THERE ANY CHANCE OF YOU AIMING AT THE TARGET PLEASE !?...

Years later, as RSM of the Depot, he put a whole coachload of school cadets in the Guardroom for having long hair. 'They've come to hear about the opportunities for a commission in the Parachute Regiment', said someone. 'I don't care if they've come to whistle Ave Maria,' said Chalky, 'if their hair is that long they belong in the Guardroom.' The Regimental Colonel, who was waiting to address the cadets, was left kicking his heels until this was all sorted out by an embarrassed Adjutant.

Worse was to come. Her Majesty was to present new Colours to four Battalions of the Parachute Regiment at a complex Parade. The Regiment's principal priorities involve training for war and to carry out a complicated Parade in the presence of the Sovereign is not one of the things they do often. As the Senior RSM, Chalky was responsible for the format of the Parade and after the umpteenth change of plan, the Regimental Colonel became concerned that the event was not going to be the credit to the Regiment that it ought to be. He consulted the Pioneer Sergeant who had been in the Regiment since before the flood and was wise in the ways of eccentric Sergeant Majors. 'Don't worry,' he said, 'he'll throw a bloody great wobbler any minute now and resign on the spot – just be ready to process it when he does.'

Sure enough, within 48 hours Chalky was massively irritated by the inability of the Colour Parties to get the timing right. 'That's it,' he said, 'I resign.' The Adjutant appeared from nowhere with a pen and the appropriate Army Form. 'Just sign here RSM', he said – and to maintain his dignity, Chalky signed. The Adjutant had a dispatch rider with his motorcycle all warmed up immediately to hand. 'Take this to the Records Office,' he ordered 'and don't come back without a receipt.'

With all his years of service Chalky was able to resign without notice and hence his resignation was immediately actioned by the Record Officer. When he formed up to withdraw it next day, saying that it was all a terrible mistake, it was too late. He had the good sense to retire gracefully and the Presentation of Colours, under his successor, was an unqualified success.

COMMUNISTS HAVE NO SENSE OF HUMOUR

Unusually for a Parachute Battalion, 1 PARA was stationed in Berlin in the mid-seventies, as a natural break from forming part of the 'Fire Brigade', as 16 PARA Brigade was called, in darkest Aldershot.

Owing to the vagaries of geography, their Berlin Barracks was not only close up against the Iron Curtain but part of it was actually on what was technically part of the East German territory.

Two Watchtowers had been built into the famous Berlin Wall which overlooked 1 PARA's Barracks and were the source of particular activity in the early morning when the Battalion fell in for muster parade, appearing to be manned entirely by East

German officers with high-powered cameras.

The RSM put up with this for a few weeks and finally produced a blackboard under the charge of the Provost Sergeant, which was angled at the two Watchtowers. After getting his Parade State from the Companies, the RSM would have the Board completed to show:

THREE MEN ON LEAVE
TWO SICK
ONE IN THE GUARDROOM
OTHERWISE 1 PARA ALL PRESENT AND CORRECT

After a couple of days of this the enthusiasm of the communist watchers visibly waned and their duty watch returned to its normal complement.

Trust a Parachute RSM to get the better of the opposition.

NOVELTY ACTS CAN CAUSE PROBLEMS

One of the many duties of the Regimental Colonel of the Parachute Regiment is the overall control of the free-fall parachute display team, the famous 'Red Devils'. The team is composed entirely of volunteers from the Parachute Battalions who have shown a special aptitude for free fall and who join the team for a tour of two or three years, sometimes returning later in their careers for another spell.

The Red Devils act as a splendid advertisement for the Regiment – and the Army – mingling with the multitudes at Displays and Shows and impressing all those who care to notice not only with their technical skills as the premier military parachute team, but also with their personalities. 'What a confident bunch of chaps.' 'What an interesting and exciting life they lead.'

Getting into the unisex business early, the Red 'Freds', as they are known in the Regiment, secured the services of a WRAC Corporal who was posted to the Regimental Depot as a telephonist. Having shown a particular aptitude for free fall, Corporal Jackie was made a full team member and later became both a stick leader, as a Sergeant, and a ladies international parachute champion.

One of the novelty acts worked out by the innovative Team

99

Commander was for Jackie to jump from the Islander aircraft closely pursued, in free fall, by the largest member of the team wearing a gorilla suit. They gyrated across the sky in a simulated chase and the gorilla almost caught up with Jackie (but not quite).

This act, which they did supremely well, always drew great applause from the crowd – until the performance at the Stowe Horse Show. The weather was marginal but rather than disappoint the crowd the Team Commander decided to go. All went well until the final act when Jackie jumped, closely followed by a LCpl wearing the gorilla suit. A sudden wind change blew them both off course but while Jackie was able to make the arena, just, there was no way that the LCpl could do so. Experienced chap that he was, he looked around for a patch of level ground and made straight for it. It so happened that this was the extensive lawn of the vicarage where the vicar's wife was taking tea with a large number of ladies, forming some committee concerned with good works, no doubt.

The unexpected arrival in the midst of this assembly of a gorilla by parachute caused something more than a stir. Worse was to follow. The gorilla suit zipped up at the back and you couldn't get out of it without assistance. The LCpl, having divested himself of his parachute harness, moved towards the horrified ladies asking that one of them unzip him. Sadly, he neglected to remove the gorilla head and his vowels were thus so distorted as to be unintelligible.

The prospect of a parachuting gorilla was bad enough but when he moved towards the assembled ladies uttering fearsome grunts and pointing to his back, it was really too much. They fled in terror. It all came good in the end when one lady, clearly braver than the rest, was persuaded to release him from the suit.

Subsequently the gorilla act was dropped from the Red Freds' repertoire. The potential for a Public Relations disaster when things didn't go right was too great.

PUBLIC RELATIONS OFFICERS ARE ALWAYS SUSPECT

There are always those officers which their Regiments feel can be 'spared', and the Parachute Regiment is no exception. Some are banished to continually attend courses and hence become known as 'coarse officers' but it is sometimes necessary to find a more permanent solution for others.

Once upon a time this was a simple matter. They were sent to the Malay Regiment, who habitually shot their officers every six months or so, which solved the problem. Then they 'Malayanised' and maybe they still shoot their officers regularly but no one ever hears of it.

The problem then recurred in the British Service of what to do with their 'spare' officers. In the fifties it was easy; they were made Recruiting Officers, which, in the days of National Service, was a relaxed backwater. Then National Service ended and recruiting became a hot potato overnight – so another repository for the unemployable became necessary.

After a false start in emergency planning where the deficiencies of the inefficient were quickly exposed by the very sharp County Emergency Planning Staffs, they finished up in Public Relations – where they still are. (Who else could have dreamed up the term JEWTs (Jungle Exercises without Trees) for troops training for the tropics on the bare ridges of Salisbury Plain!) If you ever meet an Army Public Relations Officer, treat him with suspicion – if he could do a proper job he wouldn't be in PR.

"What's the point of my staying on in the
Army if we're going to row every time I'm
late in the morning"

101

12

Nuances in NATO

KNOW YOUR ENEMY

Course 47 at the NATO Defense College in Rome had the standard international mix of members about the rank of Lieutenant Colonel, ten Germans, nine British and small numbers of the other NATO nations including a Portuguese Naval Commander who appeared to speak no known language.

Each 'committee', as the groups of 10 were called, had a similar mix of nations and committee No 6, supervised by a Turkish Diplomat, comprised two German Officers, one a civilian Scientist and the other a Navy Commander, a US Army Artillery Colonel, a Norwegian Air Force Air Defence expert, a Dutch Tank Colonel, an Italian Air Force Lieut Colonel, a Danish Infantry Officer and a Brit who had formerly been Regimental Colonel of the Parachute Regiment.

The first discussion, to break the ice and to enable members of the committee to get to know each other hinged on what each would do if the worst happened and WWIII looked imminent.

The American spoke first and said, in his Southern drawl, that he would 'act-tee-vate' 18th Airborne Corps and move it to Europe'. The Brit mumbled about getting the Queen's Order signed so that the TA could be mobilised, but the piece de resistance undoubtedly came from the Dutch Officer whose forces are heavily unionised. 'Ay vould send for the Corporal in Headquarter Kompanie who is my union representative – and Ay vould shoot him!' The British Colonel told this funny story to Clive Jenkins in later life – he didn't think it was at all funny!

THE LOST TURK

The NATO Defense College were privileged to visit the New

World to increase their understanding of how the United States and Canadian Governments and their Armed Services functioned on their home ground.

Their first visit was to Canada, where at that time Pierre Trudeau was having a dispute with his partner and the Services were going through a period of low profile. The result was that the Course got smashed for four days, with the able assistance of their Canadian minders, and when they finally departed from Ottowa at 0400 hrs to travel via Chicago and Denver to Cheyenne, Wyoming, they were not at their best. After three breakfasts, no lunch and a severe case of jetlag, the Course eventually arrived at Denver, Colorado, prior to travelling by bus to Cheyenne to visit Strategic Missile Command (presumably to pat the missiles and say 'Nice Missile. Don't go until we tell you!' – or words to that effect).

At Denver, they were met by a posse of bright young missilemen from the US Air Force. Someone explained that the Course had an arrangement for its two halves to travel, one in a Smokers' Bus and the other in a Non-Smoker. This failed to impress the boys in blue who said, with punctilious politeness, 'Sir, we don't give a s...t how you've done it before. You're now in the hands of the US Air Force. A to H in one bus and N to Zee in the other, please, SIR.' After a bit more ineffectual haggling, the Course gave up and divided into an A to H and an N to Zee bus, with the obvious results that no one knew if anyone was missing.

On arrival at Cheyenne, some two hours later, more drink was produced and just as the Course was slipping into alcoholic oblivion someone said, 'Hey, count the Turks.' So someone did, 'One, two, three – three, two, one. Total three. There should be four.' 'What is your conclusion?' asked another. 'We've lost one of the bastards.' The last time anyone could remember seeing him was in the loo at Denver Airport, so one of the Course, who was fortunate enough to possess a Hertz Credit Card, rented a car and drove back 200 clicks to Denver expecting to find the missing Turk trying to hitch a lift. Not a bit of it. When he got to Denver the drink had taken affect and he paid a quick call at the loo. There was the Turk sitting cross-legged and brooding. 'What on earth are you doing here?', he was asked. 'Well,' he replied, 'I came from lavatory and realise all my friends are gone. I not speak

English so good, so I pluck sleeve of passing lady and say, 'Ma'am, I am Turkish Officer from NATO.' She replied, 'NATE-OH. Aint' that somethin' to do with Israel?' 'At this point I realise Denver a long way from Iron Curtain. I return to lavatory to wait. My race is patient. Somone will come – I was right, you have come.'

On rejoining the Course he quickly made up for lost drinking time and finally announced to no one in particular, that his country was poor, even poorer than the British, and never would he have the opportunity to visit the New World again. He, therefore, proposed to make his visit memorable by having a white woman, a black woman and a Red Indian woman, but not necessarily in that order.

Due to the screw-up in the Denver loo, he never really got going in Wyoming where they're knee deep in Red Indians but he reported partial success at the next stop, which was Washington DC, where the Course was briefed interminably by the Pentagon, the State Dept, the CIA, the British Embassy and Uncle Tom Cobley and all. 'How'yr doing?' asked someone of our favourite Turk. 'White woman, black woman, no problem,' he replied, 'but can't find bloody Red Indian!'

The next stop was Norfolk, Virginia, to visit the Atlantic Fleet, where they went fresh out of Red Indians in the seventeenth century after a massa-cree by a particularly blood-thirsty group of colonists, and finally on to New York. After a morning listening to a debate at the UN, the Course were dismissed and told to be at JFK Airport that evening for the overnight flight back to Rome. The Turk by this time had all his mental antennae in action. 'If there is Red Indian in New York, I'll find her', he declared and set off in a fast taxi. He re-appeared just before the flight was called, metaphorically tucking his shirt in. 'Success?' asked someone. 'No, couldn't find Red Indian. Had to make do with f...ing Puerto Rican.'

The Course dispersed on Christmas leave on returning to Rome and when it re-assembled in the New Year someone said, 'Hey. Count the Turks – one, two, three – three, two, one. We've done all this before' – then to the other Turks, 'Hey fellows, where's Memhet?' 'Oh, we think you call it, in English, social disease', they replied. About a week later Memhet re-appeared. 'Caught

104

Clap,' he announced, 'must have been that f...ing Puerto Rican.'

The sequel came some ten years later at an Annual Reunionin Rome. One of the Staff approached those members of Course 47 who had managed to make it. 'Wasn't Memhet on your Course?' he asked. 'He came back last month to give the Turkish Presentation. He's now a General!'

There must be some rewards for living life to the full!

TA TRAINING IS TOUGH - MUCH OF IT IS PRACTICAL!

STAFF SYSTEMS CAN BE COAXED

The British contribution to the NATO Alliance was not too great in terms of numbers. Before the collapse of the Warsaw Pact, the United States kept two Army Corps in Europe and the Federal German Republic provided three to the British one. Nonetheless, the UK contributed subtantially to the staff system and its influence therein was out of all proportion to the force levels it provided.

Thankfully, the language of NATO is English, although technically French is an alternative. However, the withdrawal of the French from the military command structure of the Alliance in

1967 reduced the numbers of those who used French as their native tongue to the Walloon speaking areas of Belgium, less than half its total, and hence virtually all the business of NATO is based on the English language.

It is not given to every one to speak English fluently, particularly some of our American Allies, and the other nations tend to make use of the acknowledged skill of the British to write in their own language by insisting they act as recorders in joint staff meetings. 'However did the Brits get away with that?' was not an unusual observation. A glance at the foot of the paper would show that it was written by Lieut Colonel X, Royal Artillery. That's how it was done; the Brit slanted the paper to suit his own purpose when writing up the minutes of the meeting.

Influence depends to some extent on the individual's appointment within NATO, which, like any bureaucracy, has developed its own staff systems and procedures; even its own civil service. A Branch Chief can get away with a degree of initiative which would not be acceptable in a desk officer. One particular British Branch Chief always kept a stock of British Army woolly pullovers and NBC (Noddy) suits. If he wanted something from an American Officer, who are always anxious to acquire a woolly pully, he would call at his office. 'Perhaps you would like one of our pullovers, Colonel. If it doesn't fit I'll swop it for one that does. Now Colonel, about those three C130 Aircraft for that exercise in May . . .'

To a German Officer it was a noddy suit. The Germans are practical people who wished to survive in a nuclear war. Their own noddy suit was rubbish in comparison with the British version. 'Herr Oberst, would you please accept one of our NBC suits. This is a Mark Two, with the hood attached. If it doesn't fit, I'll change it. Now, about those German Airforce Transall aircraft for that exercise in May . . .'

On a major exercise it was a touch more difficult since virtually the whole staff transferred their activities to the underground operations centre, known inevitably perhaps as the Fuhrer-bunker. To start a major initiative, a Branch Chief had to secure the approval of the Deputy Chief of Staff for Operations, an appointment held by three officers of two star status on a shift system. It was no good trying anything on the hotshot US Airforce

Major General, who ruled from 0800 to 1600 hrs, nor was it wise to try and put anything over on the crusty British Rear Admiral, who took over from 1600 hrs to midnight. However, the Italian Artillery General, who took the graveyard shift from midnight to 0800 hrs, was a different prospect, particularly if one spoke Italian. The Branch Chief would wait until he was a couple of hours into his shift and then appear with his operation plan in one hand and a bottle of Chianti in the other. After a couple of slugs of booze and some small talk, the British Chief would invite the General to approve the plan. 'Che e questo stronzo?' the General would enquire (what's all this s...t). 'Non importa Signor Generale. Firmalo solamente!' (Nothing important General, just sign it.) Happily, he usually did.

When the US hotshot came on again at 0800 hrs it was too late. Forces, previously tasked in preparation, had been launched on operations and the whole thing had become irreversible.

All that was only in an exercise situation. One wonders how the system would function in war.

One of the fringe responsibilities of the Chief of the Special Projects Branch at SHAPE was to act as the Supreme Commander's representative on a rather shadowy committee to co-ordinate activities in territories which might be overrun in WWII. The first meeting of this group at SHAPE followed one of the more dramatic espionage coups by the KGB, the classic 'honey trap' straight out of Smiley's People. The dowdy middle aged secretary to the German representative had been approached by a handsome East German, who was actually a Russian, and, having fallen for him, transferred details of many secret dealings over several years. When she was eventually blown following the arrest of an even higher placed traitor who spilled many beans to save his skin, she attempted suicide by jumping from a third floor window while under interrogation. Happily, or perhaps unhappily for her, she was caught in the branches of a tree and survived to face a long sentence. (Perhaps she's now been released with the ending of the Cold War.)

A spin-off from this affair was that a whole host of plans and procedures had to be changed and the meeting at SHAPE was the most convenient means of achieving this. The national representatives all went into a huddle in the card room of the Officers' Club and the Chief of Special Projects Branch, who was not privy to their discussions, was posted as lookout man/doorman/ bouncer to prevent any intrusion on their negotiations. It was a long time since the Chief had done Sentry Go. There can't be many conferences where the door was guarded by a full Colonel.

The only other brush with the 'f.....g funnies' as the committee was referred to by the SHAPE Intelligence community was in Naples, during an international exercise, when the Chief was invited to accompany the US representative who was to make contact with an even more shadowy Greek representative without the Turkish element being aware of it. A bar in down town Naples was chosen as the rendezvous and the two sat drinking very inferior vino rosso for what seemed like hours awaiting the arrival of the Greek. The Chief had expected secret signs, or at the very least a code word or phrase in the best James Bond tradition. Not a bit of it. The US representative, who was approaching 7 feet in height with a size to match and ranked as the civilian equivalent of a Brigadier General in the CIA, had a very simple technique. As a singleton entered the Bar he would seize him with an enormous hand and, thrusting his face to within an inch of the newcomer's nose would say in unmistakable Texan 'You Pap-dop-pol-is?' None of the Italian would-be drinkers chose to try conclusions and slunk off to a quiet corner where they complained volubly of the iniquities of the Americans in their country, which fortunately the CIA representatives could not understand. When the final contact was made it was something of an anti-climax. So much intelligence work is, of course. It's only in thrillers where it seems exciting.

BEWARE OF WIVES CLUBS

The UK service personnel at the Supreme Headquarters Allied Powers in Europe tended to be very Senior Officers or very junior ranks who filled positions as clerks, signallers and drivers.

The UK Wives Club was composed almost entirely of young wives with toddler-type children, many of whom had never been far away from mum and the provisions of the welfare state. Service in SHAPE came as something of a culture shock and hence the Wives Club, which gave an impression of normality, was always well supported. The problem was getting Senior Officers' wives to run it.

When the Group Captain, whose wife had been 'Chairperson', was posted to command RAF Lyneham, the Senior British Officer, a Four Star General, who had faced similar problems before, sent for a Colonel who had worked for him in Northern Ireland. 'I want your wife to help Lady Monica (his own wife) to run the Wives Club. It's no big deal. She must have done it before.' Helping Lady Monica meant in effect doing all the work but army wives are accustomed to being put upon and the transition went off smoothly. The problem came with the Christmas Party for the numerous toddlers and sub-teenagers who constituted the bulk of the UK children in SHAPE.

Christmas Parties need a Father Christmas and happily there was a US Army Staff Sergeant at SHAPE, of considerable girth, who supplemented his income at the Yule Tide by hiring himself

'BET THAT TEN TORS EXPEDITION ISN'T HALF AS
BAD AS THEY MAKE OUT!

out to act as Father Christmas at virtually all the children's parties of the various national groups. He was duly hired by the Chairperson and tasked to appear at 3 pm on the Sunday afternoon of the party to disburse presents to all the children.

On the appointed day he duly arrayed himself in the full fig of his Father Christmas kit but decided to pop into the Top Graders Club – the international equivalent of the Sergeants' Mess – for a quick one before going on to the UK Children's Party. This proved to be his undoing! Everyone who came into the Club – and it was the Sunday before Christmas – insisted on buying him a drink – with the obvious result.

At the Party itself the absence of Father Christmas became progressively more apparent as the afternoon wore on. By four o'clock the excuse that he had been delayed by snow storms over Lapland was wearing a bit thin and at 4.30 the Chairperson took the bold decision to distribute the presents herself on the premise that a passing reindeer had dropped them off on his way to another engagement.

Despite the children's disappointment, the presents were duly distributed and the party concluded. Just as the last little cherub was putting on his coat to go home, the door burst open and the burly figure of Father Christmas swayed gently into the hall, smashed out of his mind. 'Where are all the f...ing kids' he said and passed out on the floor. The Chairperson and her helpers stepped carefully over his prostrate form and departed leaving him where he was. Perhaps he's there still!

The Chief of Special Projects Branch was dispatched by the Chief of Staff at SHAPE to brief the GOC Berlin (still locked in the Cold War at this time) on a particular operation involving the SAS.

The GOC Berlin was a most distinguished Major General known as Bubbly Spot-Wimpole.

Having travelled to Berlin on the 'British Train' – what must have been the last outpost of the British Empire – with boiled eggs for tea – the Chief duly reported to brief the General.

He was ushered in to the 'presence' and told to sit down. The General talked non-stop for 45 minutes, apparently without drawing breath, then he paused, thanked the Chief for briefing him (who had yet to utter a single word) and ushered him out. (He was able to brief the chief of Staff subsequently instead.)

Happily, the operation was never needed – the wall came tumbling down.

DON'T YOU UNDERSTAND ENGLISH?

Those serving at the Supreme Headquarters Allied Powers in Europe in the late seventies became adept at using a dialect which became known as Haigspeak, after the Supreme Commander, who could address an audience for an hour and a half, with great sincerity, and say virtually nothing.

One British Army Branch Chief was handing over his desk to another Officer who was a 'true blue Brit', a term indicating that he had not served in a NATO environment before.

They were discussing a technical point when the Executive Officer (read Chief of Staff), who was a full Bird Colonel in the US Air Force, rushed in to demand a particular paper his Master had called for.

"Hey fellers,' he cried, 'you gotta help me. I gotta have this NLT COB or it'll be OBE', and rushed out.

'*What* did he say?' asked the incoming officer. 'It's very simple' replied his colleague. 'He's got to have that paper not later than close of business or it will be overtaken by events! . . . Don't you understand plain English?'

'What message?'

111

13

Command Decisions

MILITARY DISCIPLINE MOVES IN A MYSTERIOUS WAY

By the time an officer attains One Star rank he likes to think he has moved beyond the dubious joys of taking 'orders' for offences against military discipline. Not so. A Commanding Officer cannot deal with a Warrant Officer who, if charged with an offence, must be remanded for a Star Officer to deal with.

Two cases spring to the memory of one particular Brigadier. The first was a Transport Warrant Officer in charge of a staff car pool largely manned by lady drivers of the WRAC. He obviously fancied one of his drivers and after a particularly energetic session in the back seat of her own staff car was hauled in front of the Brigadier for 'conduct unbecoming'. It was not the driver herself who reported him but her fellow lady corporal who noticed the love bites on her neck. Perhaps she felt deprived! In any event, the Warrant Officer was reprimanded and forfeited his forthcoming promotion to WO Class 1, effectively halting his career. The old adage about your own doorstep still rings true.

The other case was a Warrant Officer Class One of the Army Catering Corps who had had a previous existence with the same Brigadier as the Cook Corporal in his Parachute Company in Cyprus many years before. The gallant Warrant Officer had a self drive Escort in which he had visited a nearby town to set up a weekend training exercise for TA cooks. It just so happened that on that Friday evening the resident TA battalion, were having their office party, to which the Warrant Officer was invited. Much later – and much the worse for drink – he drove back to his HQ where he hit a lamp post and burst his radiator. Appreciating he was well over the odds in alcohol, he quickly drove home and parked his Escort in his lock-up garage, arising early the following morning to re-run the accident, when stone cold sober, and reporting it to the Military Police.

The MPs were not amused. One of our patrols discovered the broken lamp post last night, they told him – and followed a trail of coolant to your garage. This idea of just having had the accident is all bull . . .

He was therefore charged with misuse and damage of public property, which, if pushed to a Court Martial might have meant a reduction in rank. The Brigadier, having known him of old, was loath to see him retire, in a few months time, on less than a Warrant Officer's pension, and hence initiated a form of what the civilian world would call 'plea bargaining'.

Emisaries were sent to the Warrant Officer with the message that if he would accept the Brigadier's award (which – it was hinted, would be a £500 fine) rather than opt – as was his right – for trial by Court Martial – that would be the end of the matter. He was sensible enough to accept and retired without a stain on his character – to run a pub!

THE SENIOR SERVICE ENJOYS ITS LITTLE JOKES

At an Investiture at the Palace in 1981, various distinguished groups to receive a decoration from Her Majesty were separated into bundles of ten, in order of seniority, and led by very beautiful officers of the Palace Staff towards their Sovereign, through a series of elegant rooms finally reaching the ante room to the Royal Ballroom, wherein the investitures take place. One of these groups comprised two candidates for a knighthood, a civic Dignitary and a Rear Admiral who was leading the military representatives as befits an officer of the Senior Service, two Brigadiers, an Air Commodore and a bunch of distinguished civilians all collecting lesser awards. Among these was the actress Margaret Lockwood, who announced to no one in particular, as the group approached the Ballroom, that she was dying for a fag and began rummaging in her handbag for the makings. The Palace Staff 'Minder' was horrified and with great difficulty, persuaded her to hold hard as the front of the little column was already at the threshold of the Ballroom, in full sight of her Majesty, her entourage and the families and friends of the recipients.

The first knighthood candidate's name was called by the Lord

Chamberlain and the distinguished Councillor, from one of the Welsh Valleys, stepped forward to receive his reward. The Minder had briefed him to go down on his left knee but somehow, in the excitement, he started to kneel on his right knee then changing his mind he tried to reverse knees, entirely unsuccessfully and sprawled at the feet of his Sovereign. The two Queen's Gurkha Orderly Officers, who up to this point had been standing like statues as only orientals can, took one pace forward in perfect unison, picked up the unfortunate councillor, dusted him off, sorted out his knees in a fairly forcible fashion and returned to being immobile statues on the right and left of Her Majesty, who, completely unperturbed, dubbed him Knight and bid him 'Arise Sir Idwald'.

Then the Rear Admiral was called. As he stepped off he turned to say over his shoulder to the Army Officer behind, 'Brigadier, your flies are undone!' As it happened, they weren't (it was just the Navy having its little joke) but the rest of the gentlemen in line could be seen surreptitiously checking their trousers. The unfortunate Brigadier, now in the lead, was unable even to do that since he was in full view of his Sovereign and the audience. He advanced on the Monarch in the semi crouch position and never has an honour been bestowed on a more wretched individual.

One of the group recounted this later to the Queen's Private Secretary over a drink. 'That's nothing', he said. 'Last year at Balmoral I was being Minder to a group of gallant Scotsmen led by a Prince of Tonga, who was in the UK on a trade mission and being knighted as part of our export drive. Apparently, in Tonga when someone receives an Honour from their Queen, he kneels before her and shouts, 'Ying Tong, Bing Bong, Wah Wah, Ugh', or something similar, while waving his arms in the air, all to indicate homage to the Crown. At this particular investiture, my group was approaching the Start Line when the second in line, a Scotsman of great distinction, suddenly grabbed my arm and, with enormous anxiety, cried out, 'Ah canna remember a worrd of the briefing. What shall Ah doo?' Like a BF, I replied, 'Just do whatever the one in front of you does.' He didn't dare say what happened thereafter – the mind boggles.

114

During the crisis in Rhodesia/Zimbabwe in 1980, the General Commanding SW District was whipped away to comand the British Elements deployed to that area to keep the peace during the transition to complete independence. As a spin-off, his Deputy was left commanding the District, which included a whole row of VIP houses in Tidworth occupied by very senior officers in transit to a new command or a seat on the Army Board, or whatever.

During this period, the most luxurious of these was occupied by no less a personage than the Chief of Army Staff, a most distinguished officer who ultimately became Chief of the Defence Staff, the very top job for a military man. On one occasion, the Acting District Commander received a call from the MOD. 'The Chief's Office wishes to talk,' said the operator. 'Wait.' The Brigadier duly waited, anticipating that, at the very least, WWIII was about to be declared and running through the mobilisation procedures in his mind's eye. 'This is the PA to the Chief,' said a charming feminine voice after a long pause. 'The ADC wants you. Wait, I'll put you through.' Another long pause and finally a voice so languid that it could only belong to an officer of the Green Jackets came on the line. 'ADC here,' it said, 'the Military Assistant to the Chief wants you. Wait.' At this point the Brigadier was convinced that something of great moment was afoot and summoned his own senior staff to await orders. 'Hello,' said an even more languid voice, at length (clearly another Green Jacket). 'The Chief wishes to speak. Wait.' Another long pause, with anticipation rising. Finally the great man himself came on the line. 'Joe,' he said, 'my lawn mower's gone wrong. Get it fixed at once,' and rang off.

How deflated can you get?

14

Reflections of a Retread

CIVILIAN LIFE CAN HAVE ITS PITFALLS

On leaving the Active List and becoming the Secretary (read Chief Executive) of a TA Association, a long-serving Brigadier was faced with a whole new range of challenges. Masterminding the administration of the TA and Cadets was relatively easy compared with the hassles over staff and with well-meaning, if sometimes misguided, trades union representatives. As so often, the major issues were 'people problems'.

Having spent a week or so with his predecessor, the Secretary 'flew solo' on Monday only to learn that his Assistant Secretary was laid low by a heart attack on the Tuesday, from which he subsequently died. By the end of the week the Works Clerk had died of a seizure and the following week one of the Cadet Executive Officers was found dead in his armchair after returning from Annual Camp.

Three in less than three weeks seemed a bit over the top, so the Secretary assembled all the key staff, 'Look, you lot,' he started, 'this is all very new to me and I can't have people dying all over the place. In a year's time I'll know what I'm on so would you please not die for at least a year. Dying is now officially forbidden.' To their great credit, not a man died and after a year's pause the Secretary was able to send round a note thanking them for their co-operation and saying that they could now die at their discretion.

The sequel came at one of the periodic meetings of all the TA Secretaries nationwide, known in the trade, not unnaturally, as the TA Mafia. A distinguished Secretary announced to the assembled company that he had got four of his lady staff pregnant. The collective Secretaries were a body of men well used to surprises. What else could they do but congratulate him on his energy. 'No, no, you don't understand,' he said. 'Perhaps I should rephrase that. Four of my ladies *are* pregnant. I've got to give them

116

maternity leave and take on temporary replacements. I can't now balance my budget and need help!' This put a different slant on the matter and some financial arrangement was quickly completed.

When the Secretary returned to his domain he assembled all his ladies, who at the time were known colloquially as The Geriatric Jet-set. He explained the delicate position of his fellow Secretary and asked that they consider only getting pregnant one at a time, although how this was achieved he left entirely to their discretion. To their great credit, this issue has never caused a problem since.

One of the principal responsibilities of the Secretary of a TA Association is sponsorship of the Army Cadet Force in his area, each based on a county and forming what is, in effect, a cadet battalion.

"OK, break for lunch at the Black Horse. We'll try again this afternoon"

As with any voluntary youth movement, the major problem is securing the services of competent, enthusiastic officers and adult instructors who become like the Pied Piper and run excellent cadet platoons. Those whose motivation is flawed or less than total tend to have platoons of less happy cadets, usually weak in numbers. However, once an officer becomes dedicated to the Cadet Movement the problem is to push him out rather than keep him going when he reaches the age limit, normally 55 although some are extended.

On one occasion the Secretary was visiting an ACF Annual Camp at Penhale which coincided with the visit of the Honorary Colonel, also the Lord Lieutenant of the County. A senior ACF officer formed up with a complaint, 'I'm being sacked,' he said, 'and I'm only 64. My Second-in-Command is a mere boy of 58. He's only been in the ACF 41 years and he's not ready!'

The Lord Lieutenant, a distinguished cavalry officer who had commanded his Regiment in WWII at the age of 23, burst out laughing and a crestfallen senior officer withdrew. As a compromise he was allowed to stay on to command the Remembrance Parade since he had given such unstinting service over so many years.

The officers and adult instructors of the Cadet Movement give an enormous amount of their time and effort for the benefit of the youth of the nation. Admittedly only five per cent of boys and girls pass through the Cadets but they get superb opportunities to develop their character and experience. It is a sad fact that the Great British Public has virtually no knowledge of the dedication of those who serve the youth of their local communities.

PEOPLE REMEMBER THE EVENTS OF THEIR YOUTH

The Secretary of the TA Association was invited to attend the Annual Dinner of the Air Training Corps Squadron at a famous Public School to address the gathering on the subject of leadership.

The Dinner was beautifully organised with all the cadets in immaculate uniforms well supported by their parents and the academic staff of the school.

The Secretary found himself seated next to the Headmaster, a Reverend Gentleman of great academic distinction. During the course of the evening, the Headmaster dropped into the conversation that he and the Secretary had met before. The Secretary forebore to make the obvious retort that all parsons in dog collars looked the same to him and pressed the Headmaster for details. 'When you were a Company Commander,' he replied, 'I was doing my National Service. You gave me 7 days jankers for being asleep in the back of the CO's staff car when I should have been the MT park sentry.' 'It was the worst mistake I ever made in the Army', he went on. 'As a result of being on a charge the RSM got to know my name and every time anything went wrong in my Platoon it was always me that he dropped on from a great height.'

Since the Reverend Headmaster had so obviously done well in his chosen calling, it could hardly be said that he didn't gain something form his brush with authority as a youth!

"I see you were in the usual state after TA last night!"

EVEN BANDSMEN CAN MAKE A BOO BOO!

One of the several extra mural activities which devolve on the Secretary of a TA Association is to be the Chairman of the local Branch of the Soldiers', Sailors' and Airmen's Families Association (SSAFA). One of the fund raising events at the SSAFA Centenary was the Beating of Retreat by the Band of a famous Regiment.

The Band arrived early from their barracks on Salisbury Plain to change and have a cup of tea before their performance and the TA Secretary was chatting casually to the Bandmaster. 'Hey, that guy's tunic doesn't fit very well. I always thought Bandsmen were most particular about their uniform', said the Secretary. 'Ah Sir,' replied the Bandmaster, 'I had to borrow him from the Royal Green Jackets and fit him up as best I could.' 'But what about that one' the Secretary came back, 'his trousers are too long and that trombonist looks as if his uniform was designed for someone else?' 'Ah Sir,' said the Bandmaster, 'I borrowed the first from the Cheshire's and the other from the Irish Hussars. You see,' he went on, 'the Battalion has just returned from a 6 week exercise in Kenya. All the Rifle Companies went up country to train but the Band stayed in Nairobi where they formed a 'liaison' with the local squatter area – and now they've all gone down with a most virulent form of Kenyan Clap. It only lasts a few days – but it's why I had to borrow bandsmen from elsewhere for this performance. They've told their wives they've got Asian 'flu. I'm happy to say, Sir,' went on the Bandmaster, 'that none of my Senior NCOs succumbed.' Which only goes to show that the Sergeants' mess is still the backbone of the British Army.

DON'T POLISH FLOORS

The Lords Lieutenant of the Counties of the South West hold a presentation of Certificates of Appreciation each year for those who have served the Crown with distinction over many years but without reaching quite the level to be recommended for a decoration.

One Lord Lieutenant held his presentation at a local TA Centre whose staff had cleaned and polished the place as befits the dignity of the occasion. The recipients were called forward individually to receive their Certificate with due decorum and all went well until a lady, who had given yeoman service in support of a cadet unit was named. This lady came forward at a rush, slipped on the highly polished floor, and disappeared under the table (at the salute) passing her surprised Lord Lieutenant in the prone position. Like Toad from Wind in the Willows, she was set upon her feet and dusted off by the Association Secretary, whose job it is to deal with such departures from established practice, and finally received her Certificate in the upright position.

The Parachute Regiment motto applies in such cases 'Utrinque Paratus' – Ready for Anything!

TIME SPENT ON RECONNAISSANCE IS SELDOM WASTED
(old Staff College adage)

A new Medical Detachment was to be opened in a remote rural area and the District Commander had induced a local Lady of great distinction to perform the Opening Ceremony. A plaque was prepared to mark this event and positioned behind the mobile curtains which were moved around to all new works.

The day before the Ceremony the Association Secretary and the Architect ran a check on all the new works and one of them pulled the curtains on the plaque, just to make certain they worked.

To their horror they read the wording which boldly proclaimed 'On 23 April 1984 on this spot Lady ? was well and truly laid'. The thought of the press seeing this 'on the day', not to speak of the distinguished Lady herself, required urgent action. The monumental mason was called off his gravestones and set to work to produce a corrected plaque within 24 hours. Happily he made it.

I DON'T CARE IF YOU ARE LOOKING FOR A MOVE, WE'VE STILL NO VACANCIES FOR 60-YEAR-OLD SOVIET GENERALS.

121

Epilogue

It's odd to be first referred to as 'the old man' when, at 21 as a very temporary Company Commander, one was responsible for some hundred souls in the Greek Civil War, a sobering experience.

Looking back on forty-five years of service, two impressions stand out. The first is the flexibility of the army wife, constantly moving during the early years of marriage, having to cope with frequent absences overseas of her soldier husband for anything up to a year, depending on the operational emergency involved (I'm off again dear, there's no money in the bank, the school fees are due, the dog's got distemper and the car's got a funny knock in the engine. Don't forget to visit the other wives and keep up their morale. I'm sure you'll cope!' – or words to that effect).

The breadwinner returns in due course to what he expects to be a hero's welcome and to pick up where he left off, with the little woman reverting to a supporting role. Hats off to the army wife. She puts up with a lot but she does it magnificently.

The main memory of serving in the forces is the enduring quality of the real hero of the piece (or peace), the British Soldier. An all-volunteer army becomes a family and a good regiment seeks to enhance that feeling of belonging. The qualities required for never ending patrolling, guarding, defending and just straight working, interspersed with occasional bursts of high excitememnt and hyper-activity are exceptional patience, discipline, loyalty, energy and a host of other things, not least of which is a healthy element of aggressiveness when this is called for by the mission. Steadfastness in the face of severe provocation, resilience in times of severe physical hardship, dogged perseverance to carry on with a difficult task just that little bit longer and, with it all, a wry sense of humour are the hallmark of the Tom. Whatever his Regiment, he is part of a family where people just do not let each other down. Loyalty is always difficult to define but it's a potent living force for those privileged to enjoy it – and it's one of the principal strengths of the British Army.

It has been said before that the greatest privilege to which man can aspire is to command the British Soldier in action. Agreed!